AF076566

THE FALL *of* CONCH FISHERIES

A Review of Conch Fisheries
Management within the Bahamas

CORDERO M. JOHNSON

The Fall of Conch Fisheries
Copyright © 2021 by Cordero M. Johnson All rights reserved.

No part of this publication may be reproduced, stored in a retrieval system or transmitted in any way by any means, electronic, mechanical, photocopy, recording or otherwise without the prior permission of the author except as provided by USA copyright law.

The opinions expressed by the author are not necessarily those of URLink Print and Media.

1603 Capitol Ave., Suite 310 Cheyenne, Wyoming USA 82001
1-888-980-6523 | admin@urlinkpublishing.com

URLink Print and Media is committed to excellence in the publishing industry.

Book design copyright © 2021 by URLink Print and Media. All rights reserved.

Published in the United States of America
Library of Congress Control Number: 2021912331
ISBN 978-1-64753-847-7 (Paperback)
ISBN 978-1-64753-848-4 (Digital)

30.03.21

CONTENTS

Preface v
Introduction 1
Literature Review 5
Sexual Maturity 7
Economic 9
Economics & Market Demand 11
Natural   Predation 15
Environmental Effects 19
Natural Predation 25
Evaluation of Marine Reserves & Traditional Fishing Grounds 27
Declining Stocks 31
Reproductive Activity 37
Methodology 41
Opercula's Potential 51
Discussions 53
Conclusion 69
Acknowledgement 73
References 75
Appendix 79

PREFACE

This book is entitled "Fall of the Conch Fisheries" and some may be indignant with such a title, however, the "Fall" doesn't mean that there is no hope for Queen conch in the future once the proper management strategies and techniques are implemented. During my younger days I remember when you could effortlessly walkout to the shoreline and retrieve conch, obtaining the resource today however has become more of a hassle. More gas Is expended in its harvest and also compressor are more heavily utilized according to local fishermen since one must travel to deeper water in more foreign parts of the ocean just to harvest. Conch can be seen much less offshore and the demand only increases across not only the Bahamas but the Caribbean.

At heart I am an environmentalist and my concern since being raised on an out-island community were this species is how do we preserve it, How do we preserve what should be valuable for us for the next generation? The answer is simple we must document and write about it and that's my contribution to the environment. For one it was difficult researching the Queen Conch (Strombus gigas) because there is no one book that an enthusiast reader can go too and discover a multitude of information about only conch. Yes, a lot of individuals speak about it and quite certainly consume it at the restaurants or even at home but if your needed then to credit their claims on decline no book can be name…perhaps a professional can be named but no book and that's where this resource comes in.

 I attained my bachelors of Science at the University of the Bahamas in Small Island Sustainability: Environmental and Ecosystems Management. This book aims at assisting Bahamas government and other countries in protecting and providing a legislative framework a for the lucrative species. Data was collection within this book conjunction with the Department of Marine Resources that was then I analyzed resulting in new finding that can assist the future of the resource.

INTRODUCTION

The Queen conch is an important part of the culinary tradition of the Bahamas and neighboring regions. The indigenous Lucayans and Arawaks Indians used queen conch in the Bahamas and Turks and Caicos Island as a principal food source (Bene & Tewfik, 2015). Local stocks were first exploited in the Bahamas around the mid- 18th century by these settlers for commercial purposes. The Haiti trade with the Bahamas was established in 1887 and lasted until 1954, The harvesting involved the use of small boats with two men; one steering (referred to as a 'keep-up man' by local) and the other diving. Often a long staff with a rake like pronged called a 'conch hook' was also used to capture conch from on the boat. Harvest was predicted at 1000 daily in the Turks and Caicos (Bene & Tewfik, 2015). The harvesting of marines resources is a lucrative industry within the Bahamas. In 2012 the landings value estimated $ 84,349,412 Bahamian dollars generated from fisheries annually. The Dominica Republic, Haiti, and Honduras recently prohibited the export of queen conch and were previously major exporters of Queen Conch in the Caribbean (Danylchuk, 2005). In 1991, Queen conch was faced with immense pressure in Venezuela and hence it was banned within the country.

In Venezuela Queen conch was subject to over exploitation and consequently the fisheries closed in 1991 (Schweizer & Posada, 2002). During 2012 the Department of Marine Resources estimated that $5,663,918 Bahamian dollars was generated from the harvesting of Queen Conch. Stoner, Davis and Booker (2009) insist that compared to the physical extent of the Bahamas (343,450 sq. km, Caribbean Regional Fisheries Mechanism (CRFM, 2006) and its population (331,000,207, est.) make fisheries management difficult. However, literature indicates that the species has undergone excessive encroachment. Bene and Tewfik (2001) states that while extreme effort is allocated on harvesting spiny lobster (*Paniliruis argus*) and queen conch (*Strombus gigas*) the values are much different. Queen conch are easily harvestable by simple free diving methods and the usage of staffs: some divers use compressors to increase harvest. Additionally, the marine gastropod is a valuable marine resource particularly for the Caribbean and the Wider Caribbean countries; the taste, flavor and nutritive value have caused and increase in market prices and demand. The increase in the level of exploitation resulted in it's listing as a member of the Convention on the International Trade of Endangered Species (CITES) on the appendix II to aid in its management (Schweizer & Posado, 2002). Its intense fishing resulted in the decline in population decline within the Bahamas according to stock assessment by Stoner, Davis and Booker (2012). An Appendix II listing in CITES raised awareness of the possibility of extinction of the species if previous harvesting practices were not changed. Of note is that the listing protects the commercial significance and continued availability of the conch meat product (Lawrence and Phillips, 2013) Moreover, Stoner Davis and Booker (2009) insisted that conch population in New Providence Island, Bahamas has diminished beyond economically viable levels.

This book presents an analysis of Queen conch lip thickness of six distant fishing grounds within the Bahamas. The data was acquired from the Bahamas Department of Marine Resources; With a goal of determining how selective fishing impact conch maturity and to provide regularity information to the Government of the Bahamas which can inform future decision making in fisheries within the archipelago. Mean LT of 15.5 aids Stoner et. al (2012) argument whilst the distance and depth determined maturity. The theory of optimal foraging was proven indicating that maximizing landings (returns) whilst simultaneously minimizing effort. Therefore encroaching on locations with which require little diving effort and fuel consumption. Results also indicate that Man-O-War Channel and Memory Rock may be capable of colonizing more encroach shallow locations (Once Undisrupted Mating May be Continuous 1:1 ratio). The study suggest that the Department of marine resources should address lack of uniformity in conch selection through standardize lip thickness (mm) at potentially 15mm; whilst studying Fishermen and Fleet Dynamics (Hilborn (1985 p. 3)) to develop understanding the interaction between exploited stocks and human activities.

(image: by Shermako Greene 2020)

LITERATURE REVIEW

The natural abundance of conch within the Bahamas has decreased due to overfishing (Stoner & Mueller 2013, Theile, 2001). Stoner, Davis and Booker (2009) advised that "Conch populations near New Providence Island have diminished below economically useful levels and conch for New Providence restaurants are now gathered from nearby Andros Islands, the Berry Islands and the more distant Abacos". Therefore, stocks are currently being depleted and measures must be implemented to secure the fishery. Interspecific competition is one of the many complex interactions that influence queen conch migratory patterns, stock density, decreasing growth rate and juvenile distribution. "Conch nursery grounds were associated with specific combinations of food production and shelter not immediately obvious in large meadows" insist Iverson and Jory (2002), (Stoner, Lin, Hanisak, 1995). Thalasia grass is a staple for queen conch and grazing impacts sea grass meadows; *S. gigas* may consume detritus and other valuable sea grass structure. These vegetative structures support juvenile and neighboring benthic invertebrates (Stoner, Ray and Waite, 1995).

SEXUAL MATURITY

Exploitation can be measured through lip thickness (Stoner, Davis & Booker, June 2014). Randall (1964) suggested that queen conch ceases its longitudinal growth just after reaching sexual maturity at approximately 3–3.5 years of age (i.e., determinate growth), when the shell edge forms a broadly flared lip. Lip measurement and meat weight are the most common conch management strategies (Avila-Poveda & Baqueiro-Cárdenas, 2006). Cala et. al.(2013) recorded the same estimate and that population or environmental factors regulate growth (Alcolado 1976, Appledorn 1988). "Shell Morphology provides important insights into the age and sexual maturity of queen conch" states Stoner et. al.(2012). Moreover, reproductive capacity is sometimes archived month after growth of a flared lip (Hesse 1976, Egan 1985, Appledorn, 1988). The recommended lip thickness for maturity within the Bahamas is determined at 15mm (Department of Marine Resources and Stoner et. al. 2012). Moreover, regulating the species is increasingly challenging. Lip thickness implementation as a control measure is problematic due to gross dissimilarities. However, it is efficient in determining the species performance (Avila-Poveda & Baqueiro-Cárdenas, 2006).

Females collected and analyzed the Columbian Lip thickness of 17.5mm (Avila-Poveda & Baquierro- Cardenos, 2006) In Barbados 50% of the population was sexually mature at the 19mm Lip thickness for both sex. Alcolado (1976) illustrated that lip thickness vary due to environmental variability between sites (Peel & Aranda, 2011). Peel and Aranda et. al(2011) researched the Peninsula and used a mark recapture method to determine growth rate. The authors calculated juvenile conch at rate of 0.24mm+ 0.005mm a day. Peel and Aranda et. al.(2011) insist that Gibson et. al.(1983) determined a growth rate of 7.2mm month (0.23mm day-1) in Belize while Venezuela an increase of 15mm month -1 (0.492mm day -1) was measured (Weil and Laughin, 1984) and in Punta Gaulan juveniles grew an average of 10mm month -1 (0.327 day -1). Each location varied in growth rate. "Shell thickness increases with queen conch age because nacre is continuously deposited on the inside of the shell, resulting in the reduced internal space for soft tissue (Randall, 1964)" Stoner et. al (2012). Stoner et. al. (2012) futher insists, "The first histological evaluations made by Egan (1985) showed that earliest maturity in queen conch in Belize occurred at 4 mm LT for females and 3 mm LT for males. Soon thereafter, population growth models developed by Appeldoorn (1988a) indicated an LTmin of 5 mm in Puerto Rico, 5–10 months following initial shell lip formation. Similarly, histological observations on queen conch with different shell lip thicknesses in St. Christopher and Nevis led Buckland (1989) to conclude that sexual maturity was not achieved until at least 10 months after the shell flare first forms. More detailed recent studies of gonad development make it clear that LT is the critical metric in evaluating sexual maturity in queen conch (Table 5). Studies from the Colombian islands (Avila-Poveda and BaqueiroCárdenas, 2006) and Barbados (Bissada, 2011) show that the LT50 for maturity is higher than previously thought, between 13 and 19 mm, and our study in the Exuma Cays indicates that LT50 can be >20 mm (Table 5)".

ECONOMIC

The Bahamian society is heavily dependent on the marine environment. The conch resources of The Bahamas contributes some $ 4.5 million in direct income to the economy which translates into 9,800 seasonal jobs to the Bahamian economy (Spade & Daniel, 2010). Socio-economic factors contributes to its overexploitation and overcapitalization. Queen conch has been a commercially viable species throughout the Caribbean for thousands of years (Sharpira, Montana, Antczak, & Posada, 2008). Moreover the market demand has increased substantially since the 1970's making it the second most important marine invertebrate and is bested only by spiny lobster (*Panulirius argus*) in the Bahamas and U. S. markets (Brownell 1977 & Rodriguez Gil, Ogawa & Martinez-Palacios, 1991). "Early research on queen conch was not directed with stock management until species suffered rapid declines, due to heavy fishing when strong market demand became apparent". Attempts were made to manage conch fisheries by a variety of legislations and to supplement declining natural stocks in public waters to improve production. For many fisheries the attempt was not very successful". "While not unique to island nations, data collection problem are greater than in larger fishing countries" (Iverson and Jory, 1997).

ECONOMICS & MARKET DEMAND

The Bahamas is a small island developing states that generated 84,349,413 $ in 2012 the Bahamas and is responsible for maintaining and providing for a large quantity of individuals within the economy; Queen conch accounted for $5,663,918Bahamian dollars in in 2012. Statistical data on landings in values: Today fisheries is a very lucrative industry and in 2012 it accounted approximately for 84,349,412 amount of Bahamian dollars according to information from the Department of Marine Resources. Whilst lobster accounted for most with 72,801,565 and conch contributing 5,663,913 snappers' 2,567,789, stone crabs 1,233,838 and finally groupers with 1,158,876 and the other valuable marine resources making up the rest of the bulk of finances in 2012. Essentially the Bahamian society is equally dependent on the marine environment as the marine environment is on the Bahamas. Prior to that this fisheries financial report are mainly the recorded quantities from fisheries processor and hence aspects such as sport fishing and ecotourism are not accounted for and hence are aspects that are externalized from the finances recorded which essentially indicates that the amount shown may be less than the actual figure. Essentially the species contribute to 4.457 million which attributes to 9,800 seasonal jobs to the Bahamian economy (Spade & Daniel, 2010). This is a major factor that contributes to its overexploitation and overcapitalization. Queen conch has been a commercially viable species throughout the Caribbean for thousands of years (Sharpira, Montana, Antczak, & Posada, 2008). Moreover the market demand has increased substantially since the 1970's and is the second most important marine vertebrate and is bested only by spiny lobster (Panuliriusargus) in the Bahamas and U. S. markets (Brownell 1977 & Rodriguez Gil, Ogawa & Martinez- Palacios, 1991). "Early research on queen conch was not directed with stock management until species suffered rapid declines, due to heavy fishing when strong market demand became apparent. Attempts were made to manage conch fisheries by a variety of legislations and supplementary declining natural stocks in public waters to improve production. For many fisheries the attempt were not very successful. "While not unique to island nation's data collection problem they are greater in larger fisheries countries" states Iverson and Jory (1997).

The pressure on the Bahamian market is expanding since other Caribbean islands are closing their export market.

THE FALL OF CONCH FISHERIES

Landings in Values (Department of Marine Resources2012: GregBethel: Sr. Fisheries Economist)

Commercial Product	Nassau Value	Family Island Value	Total Landings
Crawfish Tail	22,707,168.33	50,094,396	72,801,565
Crawfish Whole	25,980.00	91,307	117,287
Crawfish Head	0.00	0	0
Conch	3,283,903.44	2,380,015	5,663,918
Stone Crab	578,401.56	655,477	1,233,838
Nassau Grouper	374,362.75	245,995	620,358
Other Grouper	146,362.75	322,631	468,838
Grouper Filet	14,178.75	55,501	69,680
Snapper	1,526,241.05	1,041,548	2,567,789
Jacks	237,395.98	10,451	247,847
Grunts	132,412.37	48,023	180,436
Barracuda	7,835.12	4,059	11,894
Hogfish	145,802.03	72,910	218,712
Queen Trigger Fish	31,445.00	24,723	56,168
Other	41,876.88	49,166	91,043
Total Value	29,253,210.85	55,096,202	84,349,412

Total Recorded Landing by Weight (LBS.) & Value (BS): 1980-2013

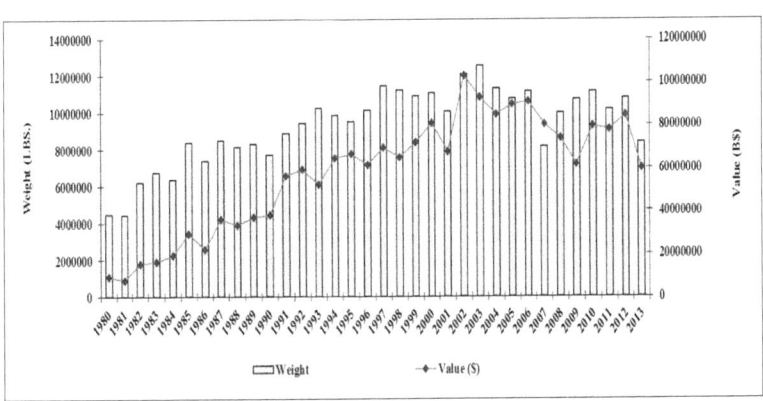

Table of Product Landings from 1980- 2013

13

Table 1: Queen Conch Meat Weight Landings and Exports

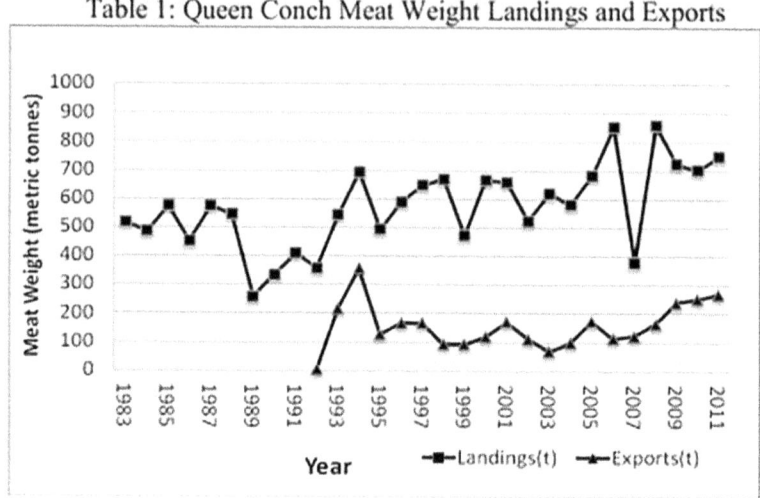

Gitten&Braynen (2009) Gittens&Braynen (2009)

Table 2: Value of Exports

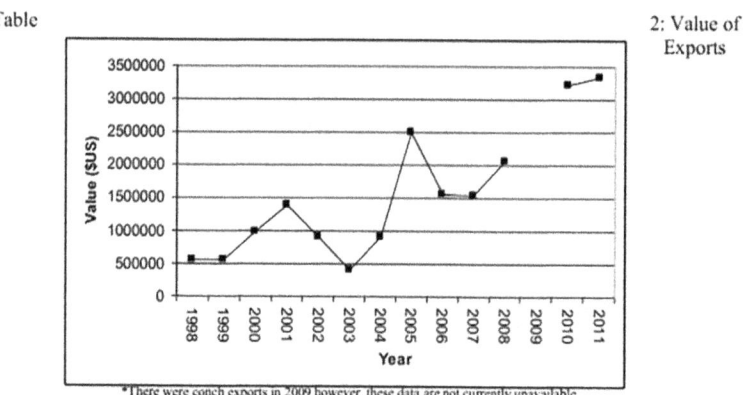

*There were conch exports in 2009 however, these data are not currently unavailable

NATURAL PREDATION

Iverson and Jory (1997) indicated that John E. Randall (1964) was the forts to provide a research paper that listed the predators of conch. Research conducted by the University of Miami in the Berry Islands during 1980- 1988 was the first to provide a thorough list of predators that consumed conch at various stages and the predators are inclusive of gastropods , crustaceans, fish and marine turtles (Iverson and Jory 1997). Iverson and Jory (1982- 1980) also conducted studies on predator based on size, the importance of shellfish strength, the difference of shell strength in varying geographic areas, hatcheries and selective predation during this same time period (Jory, 1982; Iverson and Jory, 1985; Iverson et. al. 1987; Jory and Iverson, 1983; 1985; 1988; 1988; Jory et. al 1984). Research suggest that most young and smaller conch suffer from higher levels of predation (Jory and Iverson, 1983; 1988 Iverson et. al. 1986). "Post larval settlement mortality is high regardless of where conch settle within seagrass gradient, and predation is the most important mechanism influencing conch distribution (Ray and Stoner, 1995a, Ray and Stoner, 1995b). Complex interaction are influenced by interspecific competition such as density dependent decrease in growth rate may impact juvenile distribution. Iverson and Jory (2002) admits, "conch nursery grounds were associated with specific combinations of food production and shelter not immediately obvious in large meadows (Stoner, Lin, Hanisak, 1995)". Naturally queen conch feed on thalasia grass and have a community impact on seagrass meadows and may consume detritus and other important components of sea grass beds ecosystem; their vegetative structure typically provide food for juvenile and other benthic invertebrates (Stoner, Ray and Waite, 1995). This essentially indicates that if too many queen conch are on a site there may be negative ecological impacts. " Conch predators use various methods to attack conch. Predatory gastropods forcibly enter the conch shell through the aperture to feed on the soft tissue by rasping with the radulae. other species such as calapid crabs, spiny lobsters resort to peeling and chipping on shell in a characteristic spiral pattern to reach the soft tissue (Jory, Iverson and Davis, 1992). Crushing predators is probably the most important source of predation-related mortality in small conch (< 55mm) Jory and Iverson, 1983; 1988b).", states Iverson and Jory (2002). Typical conch predator are species of gastropods, cephalopods, decapods, teleost fishes, elasmobranch and marine turtles (Randall, 1964; Jory and Iverson, Weil and Laughin, 1984; Iverson et. al 1986). Iverson and Jory (2002), states, " realistically there are probably many species that prey on conch that have not been reported that may be species that can detect and attack young conch buried in the substrate or in their nursery habitats".

Schweizer and Posada (2002) Stocks Assessment in Venezuela: Los Roques

THE FALL OF CONCH FISHERIES

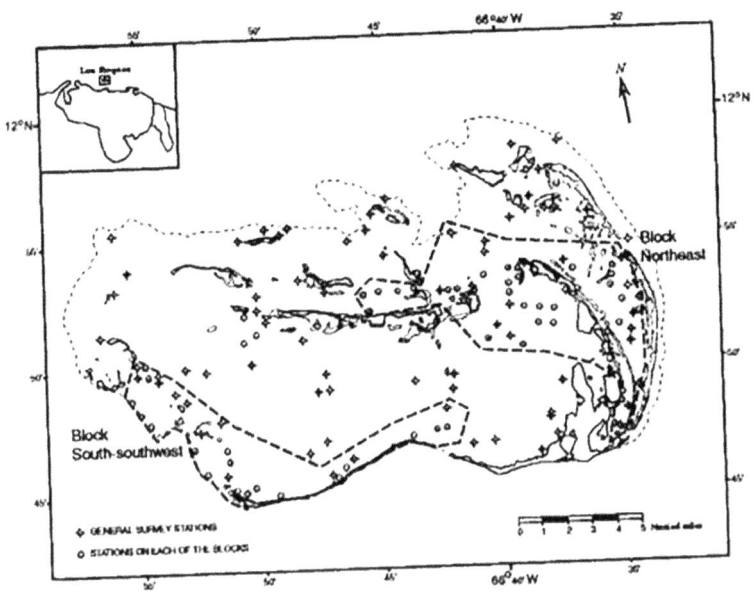

Figure 1. Location of different sampling stations visited on each of the surveys conducted in the Los Roques Archipelago National Park

Schweizer and Posada (2002) states that "at each station two scuba divers carried out visual consensus, swimming over a transect fixed width. The transects were of variable length, but a where a variable length, but a fixed time of 20 minutes".

Age Class Distribution Chart of the Queen Conch population on each of the survey conducted in Venequela, Los Roques Archipelago National Park

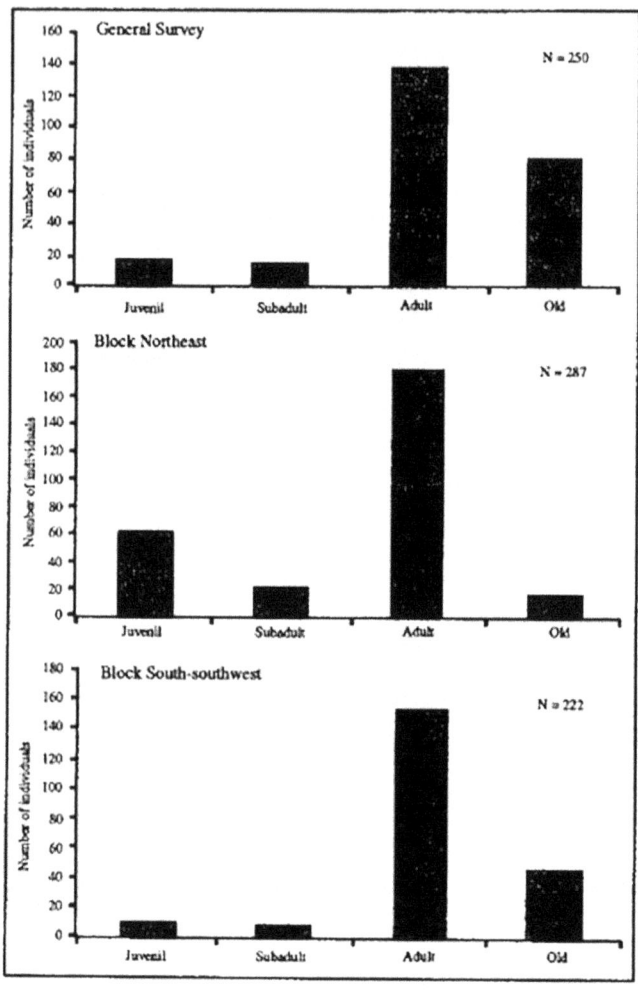

Figure 2. Age class distribution of the queen conch population on each of the surveys conducted in the Los Roques Archipelago National Park.

Shweizer and Posada (2002)

ENVIRONMENTAL EFFECTS

Reproductive activity is affected by, yearly daylight variation, photoperiod, temperature, food availability and ecological interaction (Martinet & Mondain-Monval, 1991). During the rainy season when temperature is was higher Cala et. al(2012) discovered reproductivety increased. The quantity of aggregations depicts a direct relationship between mating frequency and photoperiod; when daylight exceeded 20 hours most group of organisms mated. Aggregation per zone can be related to mating (Brownell & Stevely, 1981) and hereby connected to food abundance and substrate features as oppose to solely reproduction (Cala et. al., 2012; Alcolado, 1976). Cala et. al (2012) examined the effect of density, photoperiod/light, fishing pressure and environmental factors on mating of the conch within seasons (rainy, dry and cold front period) in Cabo Cruz, Desembarro del Granma National Park, Cuba; the highest mating frequency was discovered within the rainy season (36%) whilst dry (9%) and cold front (5%) accumulated much less. Cala et. al,(2012) discovered intense mating activity in Cabo Cruz, Cuba with year round reproductive activity which guarantees stable recruitment and sustainable populations. The author applies Appledorn (1988) hypothesis that "copulation stimulates oocytes development and maturation, leading to more frequent spawning". Predation is another factor that affect the spatial distribution of queen conch along with the quality of the habitat (Glazer and Kidney, 2004; Stoner and Waite, 1990; Marshall, 1992). "Forage (Stoner and Waite, 1990) hydrology (Jones, 1996; Stoner et. Al., 1996a) Sediment organics (Stoner et. al., 1996c)" may all be attributing factors. Distribution cannot be fully explain through habitat type but perhaps "synergistic effect of habitat with other variable "(Glazer and Kidney, 2004).

Determining maturity varies since gastropods are typically affected by environmental conditions and geography; Stoner et. al.(2012) insists "the species has determinate growth and reaches maximum shell length before sexual maturation; thereafter the shell grows only in thickness". Inferring that even though a conch have a shell length prerequisite it's soft tissues are still growing and sexual maturity based on the size of the shell may not be accurate. Moreover, location can affect maturity: in Puerto Rico lip thickness (LT) is accumulated at an average of 17- 18 mm per year (Appledorn, 1988). However, to arrive at a lip thickness (LT) of 20mm in the Bahamas the duration time is typically four years (Stoner et. al, 2012). Asserting the evidence that growth rate is dependent on environmental factors, Randall also emphasizes that larger conch produce larger eggs and higher survivor-ability (Randall, 1964). Fishing pressures can be indicated by a decrease in lip thickness; as was discovered at Waderick Wells, Exuma where the average lip thickness decrease from 15mm to 9mm (Stoner 2012). This change occurred during the period1994 to 2011 Iverson and Jory (1997) suggested that many central Atlantic countries since the 1980's have placed emphasis on mariculture through establishing hatcheries most of which have failed. Casraseal et. al.(2014) insists that despite efforts to preserve the queen conch culture, but it is faced with various issues such as seeding, feed production and infectious diseases. Iverson and Jory (1997) predicted that during the summer month's queen conch grew twice as fast.

Glazer & Kidney (2014) studied reef sites in the Florida Keys discovering various disparities in locations; the conch didn't prefer seagrass but rather rubble and tine sand which was the as opposite to conch site selection in the Bahamas . For this reason compressor are used to harvest these deep water species. Sound management of *S. gigas* require ecological and biological knowledge of the species which includes population, density, structure and growth rate (Peel & Aranda, 2011). Queen conch have large individual growth rate variation at the subset of 100-149mm shell length (Peel & Aranda, 2011). Stoner et. al. (2012) addressed both the mating frequency and density of mature conch within their research paper stating that recruitment of adult queen conch (*Strombus gigas*) adversely affect the fisheries. Therefore, to ensure a 'stable fishery' there must be sufficient adult spawners. The study was conducted in the Bahamas at traditional fishing sites in the Berry Islands, Andros Island and Exuma Land and Sea Park. It was acknowledged that recruitment overfishing of mature populations resulted in stock decline and phenotypes changes. Thus generating a question on whether to selective fishing and removal the larger species affect fisheries within the Bahamas.

Stoner et. al. (2012) studied locations within Exuma Cays, Bahamas illustrating the productivity of conch stocks within the zones. The studies indicated that the population within Lee Stocking Island has suffered drastic decline over the last 20 years and has species are rare; moreover. The authors that marine protected areas may not reach their full criteria if its design as a result of poor management. Stoner,

Mueller, Brown-Peterson, Davis, & Booker (2012) analyzed the relationship between shell length and the thickness in Exuma Cays, Bahamas, attempting to address the queen conch (*Strombus gigas*) sexual maturity through studying the gonado-stomatc indices. The general consensus was that larger queen conch both in length and width will naturally have a higher fecundity. Indicating that both size and fecundity is variable which makes setting a criteria for legal harvest difficult. Although basing laws on lip thickness is potentially easier institutionalized it doesn't guarantee sexual maturity.

Mueller and Stoner (2013) assessed the relationship between the operculum dimensions and the lip thickness to determine maturity and age in queen conch (*Strombus gigas*) within the Bahamas. Mueller and Stoner (2013) determined that the operculum is another macroscopic feature that was 86% accurate in indicating sexual maturity and age within the Bahamas: Exuma Keys, Lee Stocking Island and Waderick Wells. However, an inverse relationship between the operculum width and length and lip thickness using 15mm was the breakpoint for maturity. It's impractical to use the operculum as a regulation method because the operculum of conch is retracted when threatened by predators.

Bene and Tewfik (2003) analyzed the impact of marine reserves as it relates to density on queen conch. Bene and Tewif (2003) addressed the effect on queen conch biology that reside within the marine protected area. Moreover, conch species experienced low growth rate at higher population density. Furthermore, a spillover effect was hindered by physical barrier (long sand dunes) and predation or harvesting of isolated stocks within the Turks and Cacois Islands. Their concept was that stocks would diffuse from reserves to natural fishing areas; which would improve fishing yield. Shallow water between (0-20ft) of varying environments, sandy, mixed algal, substrate and sea grass beds which provides food and shelter were typical productive conch habitats in Turks and Caicos(Bene & Tewfik, 2003; Randall, 1964; Stoner & Waite, 1990; Ray & Stoner, 1995, Tewfik et. al. 1998). However, deeper waters (> 20m) were recently observed extensive population of Queen conch (Bene & Tewfik, 2003, Bene & Tewfik, 1996; Tewfik, 1996). The export market of queen conch experienced a rapid expansion within the Caribbean, however, over exploitation has decreased the amount of conch population predominantly in shallow nearshore communities; these stock are easily harvested via free diving and SCUBA and hookah equipment (Bene & Tewfik, 2003; Berg & Olsen, 1989; Appledorn, 1996) which allows previously unexploited deep water location to be harvested (Tewfik, 1996).

Conch Reproduction

NATURAL PREDATION

Iverson and Jory (1997) indicated that John E. Randall (1964) was the forts to provide a research paper that listed the predators of conch. Research conducted by the University of Miami in the Berry Islands during 1980- 1988 was the first to provide a thorough list of predators that consumed conch at various stages and the predators are inclusive of gastropods, crustaceans, fish and marine turtles (Iverson and Jory 1997). Iverson and Jory (1982- 1980) also conducted studies on predator based on size, the importance of shellfish strength, the difference of shell strength in varying geographic areas, hatcheries and selective predation during this same time period (Jory, 1982; Iverson and Jory, 1985; Iverson et. al. 1987; Jory and Iverson, 1983; 1985; 1988; 1988; Jory et. al 1984). Research suggest that most young and smaller conch suffer from higher levels of predation (Jory and Iverson, 1983; 1988 Iverson et. al. 1986). "Post larval settlement mortality is high regardless of where conch settle within seagrass gradient, and predation is the most important mechanism influencing conch distribution (Ray and Stoner, 1995a, Ray and Stoner, 1995b). Complex interaction are influenced by interspecific competition such as density dependent decrease in growth rate may impact juvenile distribution. Iverson and Jory (2002) admits, "conch nursery grounds were associated with specific combinations of food production and shelter not immediately obvious in large meadows (Stoner, Lin, Hanisak, 1995)". Naturally queen conch feed on thalasia grass and have a community impact on seagrass meadows and may consume detritus and other important components of sea grass beds ecosystem; their vegetative structure typically provide food for juvenile and other benthic invertebrates (Stoner, Ray and Waite, 1995). This essentially indicates that if too many queen conch are on a site there may be negative ecological impacts. " Conch predators use various methods to attack conch. Predatory gastropods forcibly enter the conch shell through the aperture to feed on the soft tissue by rasping with the radulae. other species such as calapid crabs, spiny lobsters resort to peeling and chipping on shell in a characteristic spiral pattern to reach the soft tissue (Jory, Iverson and Davis, 1992). Crushing predators is probably the most important source of predation-related mortality in small conch (< 55mm) Jory and Iverson, 1983; 1988b).", states Iverson and Jory (2002). Typical conch predator are species of gastropods, cephalopods, decapods, teleost fishes, elasmobranch and marine turtles (Randall, 1964; Jory and Iverson, Weil and Laughin, 1984; Iverson et. al 1986). Iverson and Jory (2002), states, " realistically there are probably many species that prey on conch that have not been reported that may be species that can detect and attack young conch buried in the substrate or in their nursery habitats".

Schweizer and Posada (2002) Stocks Assessment in Venezuela: Los Roques

EVALUATION OF MARINE RESERVES & TRADITIONAL FISHING GROUNDS

Marine Reserves aren't efficient and often don't fulfill their intended purpose especially without proper management and resources. The Bahamas has many marine reserves that are mismanaged and that doesn't accomplish its committed and purpose and a part of the reason is limited resources. Stoner, Davis and Booker (2012) have shown where there was reproductive failure within the marine reserve. "The overall population of adults have declined 35% over the last 17 years (69% in shallow bank habitats) and the adult population was significantly older in 2011 than it was in 1994; declining numbers and aging means that larval recruitment to the ECLSP has diminished and surveys for the queen conch upstream from LSI show that spawning stocks has reached reproductive failure. (Stoner, Davis & Booker, 2012). The marine resource despite being proclaimed to be protects by legislative bodies and enforcement agencies have undergone encroachment. Stoner, Davis and Booker (2012) studied traditional fishing site within the Bahamas and discovered that larger stocks are dwindling due to recruitment overfishing and selective harvesting. Stoner & Ray (1996) illustrated that the densities inside Exuma Land and Sea Park (ECLSP) and Warderick Wells when compared to Lee Stocking Island were 31 times greater in densities which showed that the fishing grounds had less species than the marine reserves. Stoner & Ray (1996) also concluded that after years after this study was completed the pressure on the resource has increased astronomically because of increasing seafood demand within the Bahamas and the Wider Caribbean. This demand has also caused unsustainable and illegal harvesting method to become more prevalent such as the capture of juveniles and the once unexploited deep water stocks that weren't harvest because of limited technology are on the agenda which affect the mature stock rating.

Table Showing Mating Probability

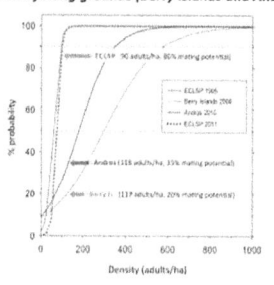

Figure 7. Statistical probabilities of observing mating behavior in queen conch in the ECLSP and in two fishing grounds (Berry Islands and Andros).

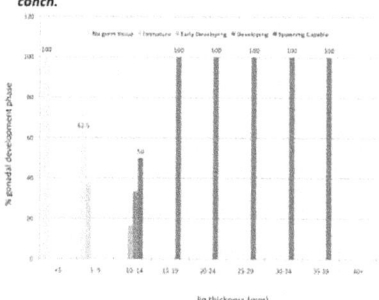

Figure 8. Percentage of gonadal development phases in ovaries by size class (mm lip thickness) for female conch.

Stoner Davis and Booker (2011)

Additionally, the survey in Andros Island by Stoner & Davis were eight tradition fishing grounds illustrated that most modest juvenile population where found in North Bite and Middle Bight whilst Grassy Cay had the most substantial mature population and however a vast majority of the population is are small and have low fecundity or reproductive potential. Therefore it was recommended that Middle and North Bight and Grassy Cay be zoned as a marine reserve. Stoner, Davis and Booker (2011) stated that the abundance of queen conch has declined astronomically over the past few decades within Lee Stocking Island and Exuma Land and Sea Park. "Density on the island shelf east of Lee Stocking Island declined 91% between 1991 and 2011. The conch their have thinner shells now and are younger, typical for overfished population. As in 1991, the population at Lee Stocking Island to the west was very low", conveys Stoner, Davis and Booker's (2011). They also insisted that mature adult conch in Lee Stocking Island have diminished by approximately 91 percent after the mid- 1990's and that Exuma Land and Sea Park is now the primary source of larvae for the Exuma Sound System and that the present population within the reserve cannot sustain itself. Stockhausen et al., Gaines et al., 2010, Kaplan et. al. 2009, all stated that the marine reserve within Exuma Cays cannot sustain a population if the neighboring environments are constantly exploited. This indicates that there was overexploitation and overcapitalization within this near shore littoral environment which vividly depicts the miss management of the species. This indicate that the marine reserve itself is encountering enormous pressure and the present surplus may not be able to replenish itself "Low efficacy of MPA's can also tarnish the legitimacy and future adoption of closed areas by stakeholders. In fact the changes in population structure of queen conch in ECLSP suggest the population is not self-sustaining" explains Stoner et. al (2012). Data suggest that the marine protected area isn't as productive those involved might loss interest or abandon all future ideas and implementations of reserve elsewhere. Danylchuk (2005) further describe the marine reserve as a 'walk in' fishery and that high levels of juveniles are harvested in Cape Eleuthera. Marine Reserve face issue of management and resources for its effective management: if enforcement officer aren't able to proper guard the facility fisherman inevitably utilize the art of optimal foraging and harvest.

Surveyed Sites; Stoner, Davis and Booker (2011)

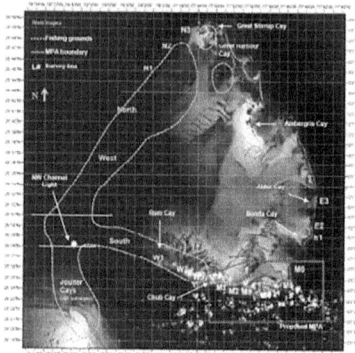

Figure 1. Map of 2009 Berry Islands survey sites.

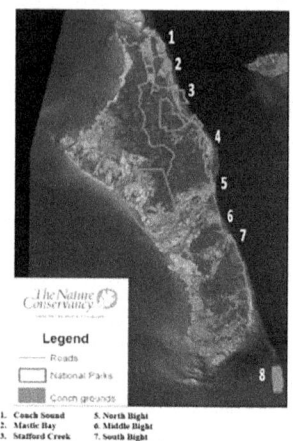

Figure 2. Map of 2010 Andros Island survey sites.

Stoner, Davis and Booker (2011)

DECLINING STOCKS

Conch fisheries have resulted in stock decline and in some cases closure. Commercial support of the valuable gastropod in the Caribbean bioprovince has resulted in habitat loss, overfishing and region wide depletions (Berg and Oslen, 1989; Appledorn, 1994) which resulted in its categorizations Appendix II with the Convention on the International Trade of Threatened Endangered Species of Flora and Fauna (CITES)(Glazer & Kidney, 2004). Venezuela, Bermuda, Haiti and the Florida Keys banned the harvest of Queen conch. During the conch fisheries closure from 1992-1997 the estimated "population from shoal-water, back reef zone throughout the Florida Key increased from 6000-21000 individuals" (Florida Fish and Wildlife Conservation Commission, unpubl. data., Glazer and Kidney, 2004). Demand for the shells, jewelry and meat lead to expansion of commercial harvest within the region (Avila-Poveda & Bacqueiro-Cardenas, 2006). Increased anthropogenic activities such as tourism development contribute to stock decline (Berg, 1976 & Brownwell & Stevey, 1981).

The Bahamian Archipelago is a part of a limited group of nations with a viable and lucrative fishery export market. Although lip thickness is a common maturity indicator and regulation method some fishermen "knock out" conch from their shells at sea: leaving the shells in the ocean. Mueller & Stoner (2013) state that processing of queen conch at sea is economically sound ventures at sea especially with smaller fishing vessels. Processing at sea decrease weight and fuel consumption especially ventures with involving small fishing vessel leads to the evidence of shell middens. Without the shell it's difficult to estimate maturity which present a unique challenge for fisheries managers.

Fisheries managers often use marine reserves as location to replenish depleted stock. However, development of a standardized lip thickness is seen as a more direct harvest management method. Mueller and Stoner (2013) however, inferred that Allison et. al. (1998) asserted marine reserves will not be effective in preventing stock decline without other forms of management. Bene & Tewfik (2003) insisted that marine protected areas are regularly promoted as viable compliment to various classical forms of marine resource management. Stockhausen et al.(2011), Gaines et al., (2010), Kaplan et. al. (2009), all stated that the marine reserve within Exuma Cays cannot sustain a population if the neighboring environments are constantly exploited. Stoner, Davis and Booker (June, 2014) quotes "It's clear that current management and regulations are not adequate to sustain conch resources in the Bahamas". Cala et. al.(2013) referred to Stoner & Ray's(2000) study indicating that the relationship between queen conch density and frequency of production and deserved no. mating at 56 adults (ind/ha). Stoner et. al.(2012) indicated similar mating frequencies at 47 and 46 in the Berry Islands and Andros Bahamas.

Stoner, Davis and Booker (June, 2014) reports that Exuma Cay, Lee Stocking Island area, the east coast of Andros and Abaco and the unprotected Berry Island Marine Fishery Reserve experienced heavy fishing pressure of which the < 10mm average indicates. De Jesús-Navarrete & Valencia-Hernández (2013) researched the declining densities and reproductive activity of queen conch within Banco Chinchorro, Eastern Caribbean Mexico whereas 15 sites where analyzed within two months of the rainy and dry season. They discovered a population decreased 30 % density in 2009 when compared to 1990. Stoner et. al (2012) concluded a similar decline in Exuma Land & Sea Park Bank at 69 % and Lee Stocking Island at 91% density from 1994 to 2011. Schapira et. al.(2009) analyzed the molestation and overharvesting of queen conch (*Strombus gigas*) within Venezuela, Los Roques Vulnerability of queen conch stocks was determined by the examination of shell middens: these middens where examined at various time frames and it was noted that some middens where created during different time spans from the pre-Colombian era to modern fisheries. shell composition from different times was dissimilar. However, regardless of the time the larger conch stock where typically the ones collected. Due to optimal foraging the middens contained mainly large shell sizes and that most the conch species level of encroachment has steadily increased over the years.

De Jesús-Navarrete & Valencia-Hernández (2013) results indicated that the sample densities where below sexual mature densities in Banco Chinchorro, Eastern Caribbean Mexico. Banco Chinchorro, Eastern Caribbean Mexico regulates based on shell length (200 mm) and sexual maturity (lip thickness 4mm width). De Jesús-Navarrete & Valencia-Hernández (2013) indicated that 90% of the exploited population were juveniles which ultimately affect the stock density(De Jesús-Navarrete & Valencia-Hernández, 2013; Berg & Olsen, 1989; Stoner et. al., 2012). In July the shell length mean average was 187.63 which was below the preferred 200mm. De Jesús-Navarrete & Valencia-Hernández, (2013) discovered that fishing pressure especially via illegal harvest contributed to density decline. Bene & Tewfik (2015) described queen as an "immobile animal found on the sandy plains that cover a large proportion of the bank". Therefore, the species require low effort and little skill to harvest (Bene & Twefik, 2015). Regular harvest depth within the Turks and Caicos for Queen conch is 20-35 ft (average of 27.5 ft, about 8m) (Bene & Tewfik, 2015).

Stoner, Davis and Booker (2012) insist that fishers confirmed selective fishing in Andros Island and the Berry Islands due to higher price of a larger queen conch species. "Sampha" conch relatively small sexually mature conch was observed at Andros Island and Barry Island site which was rare in less fished parts of the Bahamas (Stoner, Davis & Booker, 2012). Growth rate is very strongly relative in juvenile conch to habitat type (Ray & Stoner, 1994) and small size of mature conch may be a result of naturally slow growth. "Sampha" conch may have almost no spines. Despite these factors, fishing pressure may cause a reduced size at maturity (Law, 2000; Conover et. al. 2005; Hitching, 2005; Walsh et. al., 2006; Stoner, Davis & Booker, 2012). Stoner, Davis and Booker (2012) quotes "we know less about long term for exploited crustaceans (e.g. Melville-Smith and De Lesting, 2006, Zheng, 2008), and histological data exist for at least one gastropod (*Zidona dufrennei* Donnovan, 1823) showing that size-at-maturity decreased significantly over 10 yrs period of heavy fishing (Torroglosa & Gimenez, 2010).

Bahamian Conch Salad

REPRODUCTIVE ACTIVITY

Queen conch are gonochristic but exhibit sexual dimophism; the males possess a verge (penis) whilst the females have a groove (Reed 1993, Titley-Oniel et. al. 2011). *S. gigas* unlike most marine gastropods uses it's operculum to glide across the ocean floor (Mueller and Stoner, 2013). Avila-Poveda and Baqueiro-Canademas(2006) highlighted the issue that most studies face (inclusive of Randall, 1964, Alcodado, 1976; Weil and Laughlin, 1987, Wicklund et. al. 1991; Berg et. al. 1992; Stoner et. al 1992; Appledorn, 1994) using external macroscopic features of the gonad, reproductive behavior and growth models as criteria for assessing maturity. Avila-Poveda and Baquero-Cardenas (2006) determined size and maturity in the San Andreas, Archipelago, Provencia and Santa Catalina (SAI), Columbia. Glazer and Kidney (2004) states that during the summer months, adults aggregate in shallow water (Randall, 1964; D'Asaro, 1967, Brownell, 1977) In Columbia, the criteria for maturity was 5mm. However, after assesses 316 samples of microscopic characteristic to determine sexual maturity their research lead to recommendations of a 13.5 lip thickness recommendation to the Columbian government. Avila-Poveda & Bacqueiro- Cardenas (2006) focused on other fishery management tools, (resolution No.

000179 of 05 May, 1995) based on general knowledge of the species, gear restrictions, harvest quota, closed area. Previously, a weight restriction that prohibited conch weighing less than 225g without cleaning was implemented in Columbia. Unfortunately, extraction within the location had no "uniformity" and implementation of a new strategy was deemed necessary.

Spade et. al.(2010) suggested that climate change and anthropogenic impacts on the environment is inferred as one of the main reasons for heavy metal near shore (NS) and inhibits the queen conch's ability to reproduce. Glazer and Kidney (2004) states that during the summer months, adult's aggregation in shallow waters (Randall, 1964; D'asaro, 1967; Brownell, 1977). Adult queen conch is also known to undergo seasonal migration. Moreover, evidence on reproductivety (mating) spawning and egg masses is limited and scare within the Caribbean (Cala et. al., 2012).

Peel and Aranda (2011) indicated the difference in growth rate between various countries Virgin Islands, USA (4.16 mm month-1) (Randall 1964), Cuba (Alcolado, 1976) (3.3 mm month-1), Florida Keys, USA (4.5 mm month -1; Brownell, 1977) Belize (7.2 mm month) (Gibson et. al. 1983), Venezuala (15mm month month -1; Punta Gavilan, Mexico (10 mm month -1; De' Jesus-Navarette & Oliva-Tivera, 1997), Banco Chinchoro, Mexico (3.2mm month-1; De Jesus-Navarrete, 2001). Queen conch within the Bahamas undergo seasonal migration; from nutrient rich rubble communities to sand flats for reproductive purposes (Glazer & Kidney, 2014; Stoner & Sandt, 1992). A similar relationship can be seen in Turks and Caicos, where nature mature adult species migrate from seagrass dominated communities to a seagrass dominated community to sand algal community which can be attributed to the winter season (Hesse, 1979). Therefore different habitats may be utilized during reproductive and non-reproductive seasons. Glazer and Kidney (2014) and Stoner and Sandt (1992) observed that rubble and coarse habitats where preferable during non-reproductive annual time periods and Stoner and Sandt (1992) discovered a similar migratory pattern.

"Strombids possess both egg groves and pseudopenis which have been observed in two species from the Pacific Ocean, *Strombus luhunas* (Linneaus, 1758)(Kuwamura et. al. 1983) and *Strombus gigas* (Linneas, 1758; Reed, 1993; Philip, 2000) and *Strombus puglis* (Linneas, 1758; Reed, 1993)", states Tiel-O' Neal et. al. (2011). Titley-O' Neil et. al. (2011) studied the relationship of imposex within the species, suggesting that the species exhibits sexual dimorphism and are gonochoristic. Reproduction amoung *S. gigas* is seasonal whereas in copulation. The males extend his penis (verge) into the females egg grove and sperm is deposited internal fertilization occurs (Titley-O' Neil et. al., 2011; Orr & Berg, 1987). Between March and October these fertilized eggs are typically laid. On the sea floor (Davis, 2010). De Jesus-Navarrette & Valencia-Herandaz, 2013) indicated highest reproductive peak of queen conch during July. Moreover, several author asserted the peak egg laying months are between n July and September at a typical water temperature of ~ 28-30 C (Titley-O' Neil et al., 2011, Davis et. al 1984, Weil & Laughin, 1984). Mating occur at a 1: 1 sex ratio undisrupted population (Titley-O' Neil et. al., 2011; Robertson, 1959; Davis et. al. 1984).

The Bahamas regulation on lip thickness is discretionary. Therefore, this research presents an analysis of Queen conch lip thickness of six distant fishing grounds within the Bahamas, with a goal of determining how selective fishing impact conch maturity and to provide regularity information to the Government of the Bahamas which can inform future decision making in fisheries within the archipelago.

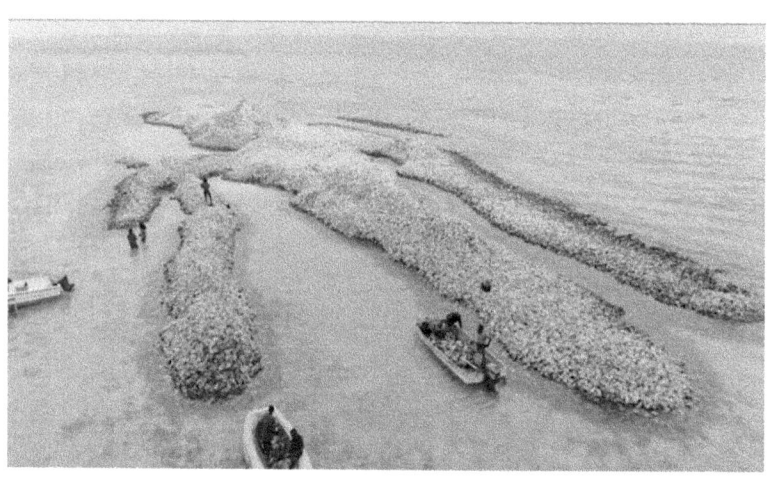
Areil View of conch shell middens (Monique Willaims)

METHODOLOGY

Study Site

The Department of Marine Resources conducted a study on conversion factors under CITES Decision 16.143, which obligated queen conch range states are obligated to adopt queen conch conversion factors by the end of 2015 and applied by the end of 2016. The data was utilized to address question in the present. Samples were collected from specific fishing ground ranging from the east, west, north and central Bahamas. Six disparate fishing grounds were sampled; East Booby Rocks (N 25 °09.247, W 077 °031221), Lower Samphire (N25 °12.232, W0.76 °58.242), Man-O-War Channel (N22 °47.322, W0.75 °53.481), Upper Samphire (N25 °10.643, W077 °00.381), Memory Rock (N26 °57.251, W079 °06.439) and Southern Long Island (N22 °51.010, W074 °51.728) (Figure 1.). The common fishing site were chosen based on varying depth and environment. The depth of the locations ranged from 6 feet to approximately 45 ft. Small powerboats/ dinghies were the transportation method to study sites. Stoner et. al.(2012) best describes these environments. The Bank environment in the study area is characterized by "broad sandy flats gradually increasing in depth from shallow intertidal areas near the island tot eh edge of the bank. These flats include coarse white sand with little vegetation, extensive meadows of turtle grass (*Thalassia testudinum*) extensive hard bottom covered with macro-algae such as Laurencia and Sargassum species and soft and hard bottom habitat are common on the bank and more continuous reef area (to several hectares)" (Stoner et. al., 2012). The areas where sampled. Physical and geographic features of the environments were recorded.

Sampling Method

The study was focused mainly on determining sexual mature population in fishing grounds at varying depth and environments. A sample size of 315 queen conch were collected throughout 2014. The samples were collected by local fishermen without any uniformity and the measurements were recorded. Freediving was the method used to gather conch. The conch view selectively chosen based on fishermen preferences. The lip thickness were observed and recorded using a digital calipers and slates. The weight was measured with an electric scale in grams (g). Determination of sex was done by observing a verge (male penis) and groove (female) and the perception on flared was recorded. Flared was defined as a deviation in normal thickness of the shell lip. The term flared was used to indicate that is utilized to indicate maturity and age. Analytically 15mm Lip thickness was used and the break point for sexual maturity. Statistically significant data where coded within Microsoft Excel and it was charted in pivot tables and bar graphs. This data was utilized to understand the environment variability and fishing pressure effects on Queen conch within the Bahamas fishing grounds. Microsoft Excel data from 2005-2010 were also recorded and analyzed from the Department of Marine Resources to strengthen the study.

Data Analysis

Statistically significant data where coded within Microsoft Excel and it was charted in pivot tables and bar graphs. This data was utilized to understand the environment variability and fishing pressure effects on Queen conch within the Bahamas fishing grounds. Microsoft Excel was utilized to generate pivot tables and graphs. Using the Box Plot, Tyler Slab.com Box Plots and Tables were created to illustrate the Upper Whisker, 3rd Quartile, Median, 1st Quartile, Lower Whisker, Sample Size, Standard Deviation and Variance (http://boxplot.tyerslab.com). Social Science Statistics' T Test was utilized to determine the significance in data. Pair treatment values were entered into text boxes (treatment 1, treatment 2) (http://www.socscistatistics.com/).

Results

Figure 1. Conch Sampling Sites

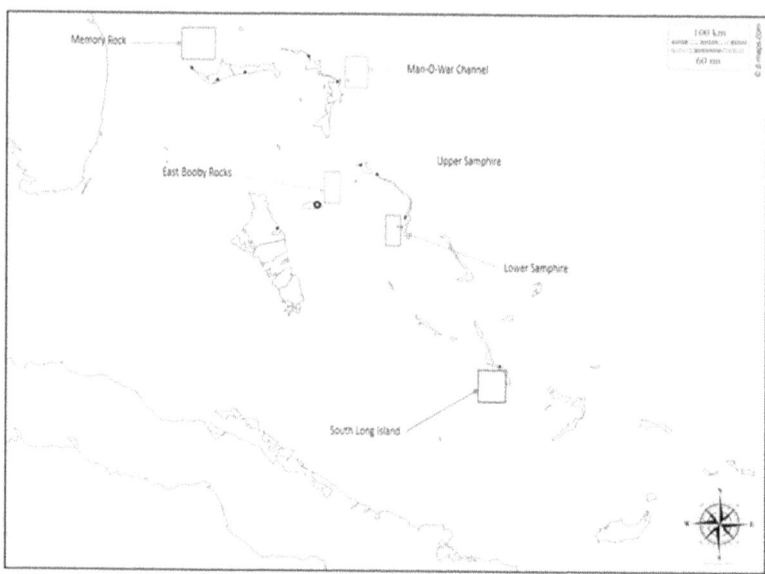

Figure 1. M

Map showing conch surveyed sample sites. These sites were color coded and is formated into the graphs and tables below.

Table 1. The Physical Characteristics of Fishing Grounds

Location	Habitat Profile	Range of Depth(ft)	Coordinates (GPS)
East Booby Rocks	Mixed Shoals/Sand Banks and Rocky	18-20	N 25 °09.247, W 077 °031221
Lower Samphire	Sandy and Rocky & Small Shoal/Sand Bar	6-18	N25 °12.232, W0.76 °58.242
Upper Samphire	Sandy and Rocky & Small Shoal/Sand Bar	6-18	N25 °10.643, W077 °00.381

South Long Island	Mixed Reef, Sandy Shoal/Bank and Seagrass	6-16	N22 °51.010, W074 °51.728
Memory Rock	Mixed Reef & Shoals/ Sand Bars	18-30	N26 °57.251, W079 °06.439
Man-O-War Channel	Sandy Shoal & Rocky	33+	N22 °47.322, W0.75 °53.481

Table 1 illustrates the range of depth (ft), coordinates(GPS), lip thickness (mm) and whole weight (g) at which samples were taken for each site. The physical characteristics of the sites were charted.

Figure 2.

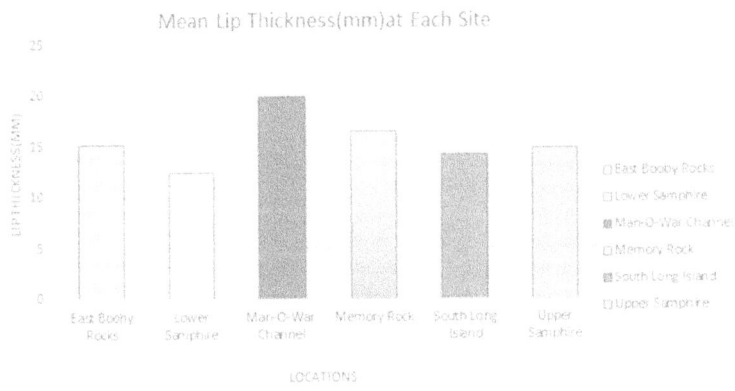

Figure 2.indicates the difference in lip thickness at locations. Man-O-War has the highest average lip thickness 19.8 mm. East Booby Rock was -0.4mm below the Mean of 15.5mm. Lower Samphire was -3.1mm below the mean. Man-O-War Channel was + 4.29 mm above the mean. Memory Rock was + 1.1mm above the mean. South Long Island was – 1.3mm below the mean. Upper Samphire was -0.8 mm below the mean. Man-O-War Channel maintained the highest distance from the mean. Lower Samphire (-3.1mm) was the lowest below the mean.

Figure 3

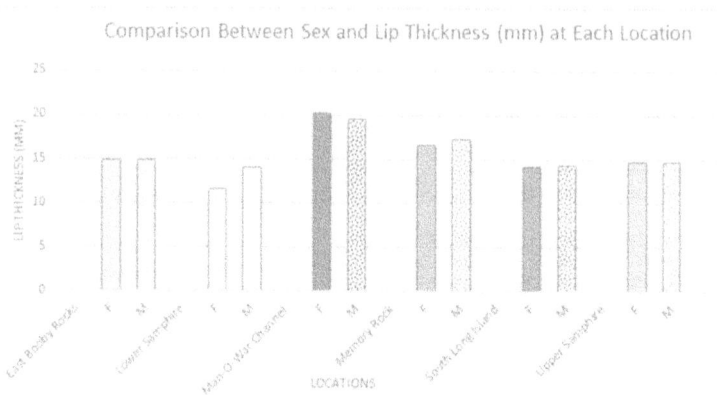

Figure 3. compared Sex and Lip thickness mm at sites. Male is represent by M and Female by F. To understand the spread a box plot was created.

Figure 4.

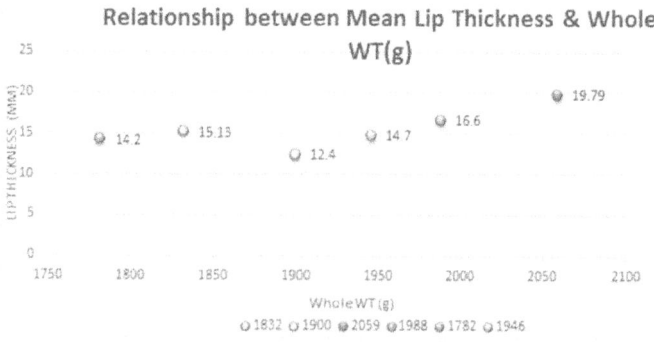

The above graph illustrated the color coded survey location and their relationship with Mean Lip thickness and Whole Weight (g). Lower Samphire lip thickness has the lowest lip thickness but higher whole weight than Upper Samphire and East Booby Rocks.

Figure 5.

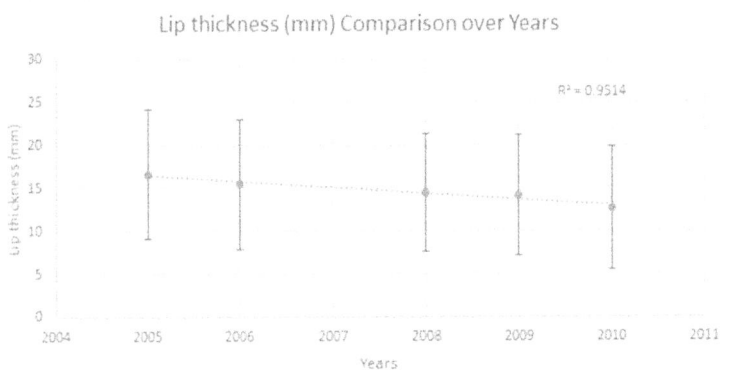

Mean Lip thickness addressed in the chart. The average lip thickness of each year was place into the chart illustrating the trend. The 2014 sample was 15.5 mm LT, the data collection method for the 2014 sample was different. Retailers are known to obtain much smaller conch from fishermen as oppose to the fish houses that require a larger size. The data for 2005 – 2010 where collected from retail vendors on Potter's Cay and Montagu. Refer to the Appendix for breakdown of Lip thickness from 2005-2010.

Figure 6.

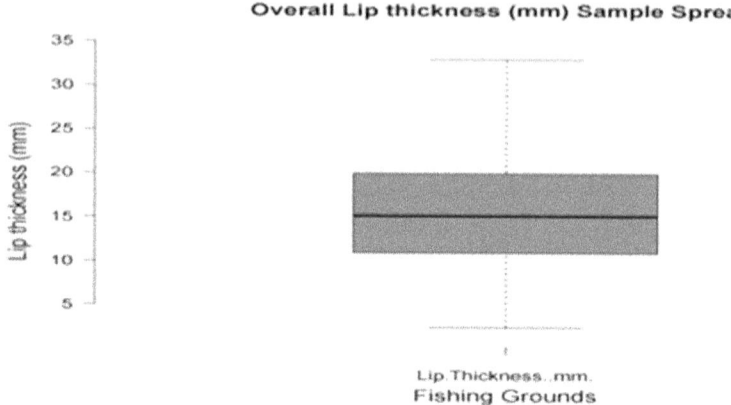

Figure 6 illustrate the population size used was 31, Median (15.2), Minimum (2.5), Maximum (33), First quartile (11), Third quartile (20), Interquartile Range (9) and Outliers (33).
(http://www.alcula.com/calculators/statistics/box-plot/)

Figure 7.

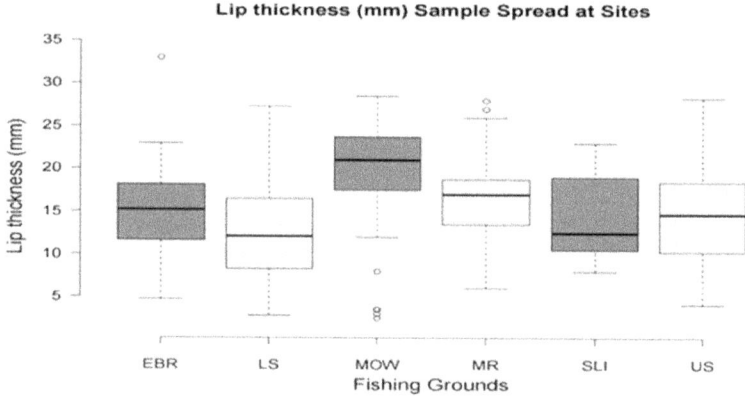

Figure 7 illustrates the spread of LT mm sample at fishing grounds. The Fishing Ground represented with the acronyms East Booby Rocks (EBR), Lower Samphire (LS), Man-O-War (MOW), Memory Rock (MR), South Long Island (SLI) and Upper Samphire (US). The acronyms are also applicable to Figure 8.

Figure 8.

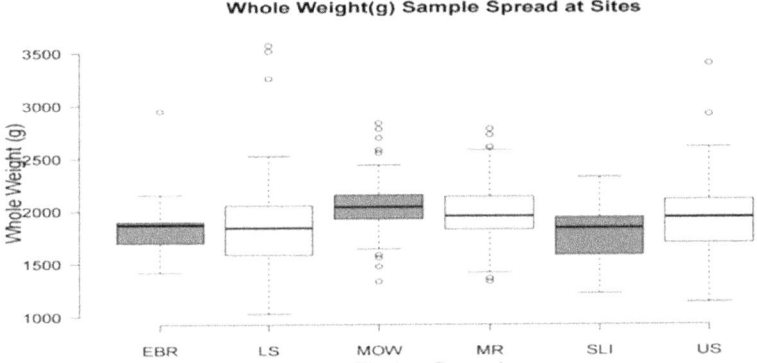

The spread of whole weight at each location is displayed in Figure 8. Figure 4 illustrates the direct relationship with Figure 7 and Figure 8.

OPERCULA'S POTENTIAL

The operculum is the portion of the conch that is referred to as the foot and it allows the snail entrenched itself and drags itself across the ocean floor. Due to the fact that queen conch may attain maturity earlier than some and that it's inverse relationship with lip thickness may aid in the determination of proper lips size criteria. The operculum can be used to successfully determine maturity: It was predicted that 86% of queen conch maturity was determined (Stoner et. al., 2012). However, the operculum may break as the conch mature and it may be impractical to use such a method considering during catch may have to remove the conch from its calcareous shell first and there operculum can only be used effectively for monitoring the maturity of the species. "Lately biologist, have begun to use gastropods opercula to game new insights into the life history of marine snails" (Mueller and Stoner 2013). Stoner et. al 2013 also explain " Sexual maturity in queen conch varies throughout the Caribbean region. In this study we used 15-mm LT as the conservative test for the Bahamas (Stoner et. al. 2012), but other breakpoints could be applied. For example 50 % percent of females sampled in selected areas of Columbia were mature at LT of 17.5mm, whereas 50% of the males were mature at 13mm LT regardless of gender (Avila- Poveda&Bacqueiro- Cadenas

2006). In Barbados, 50% of the Strombusgigas population sampled was sexually mature at 19-mm LT regardless of gender (Bissada 2011)". The general idea is that the operculum length and width can produce information on life history of the queen conch species. Moreover, the operculum length and operculum width can be put into practice since the size has a relationship with lip thickness and maturity within different zones or ecosystems and this would aid in establishing a maturity criteria.

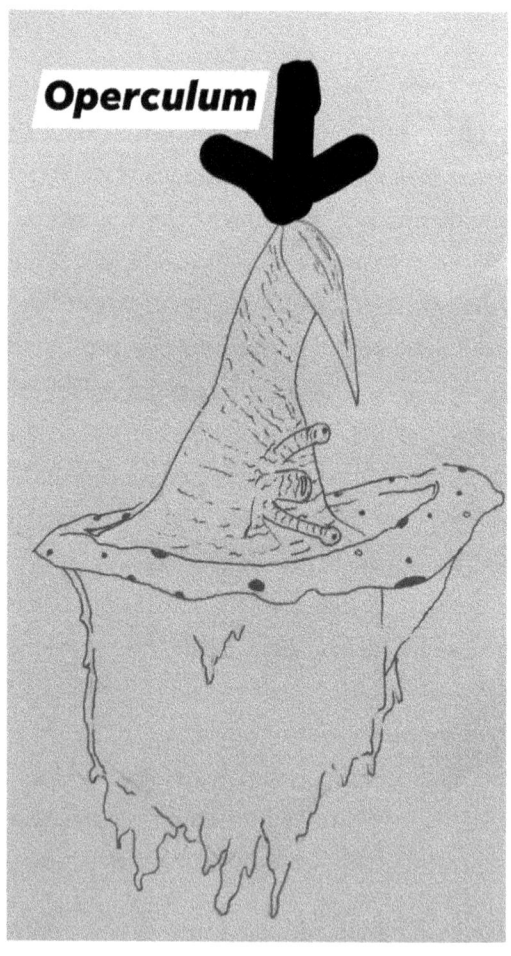

(Image by Shermarko Green 2020)

DISCUSSIONS

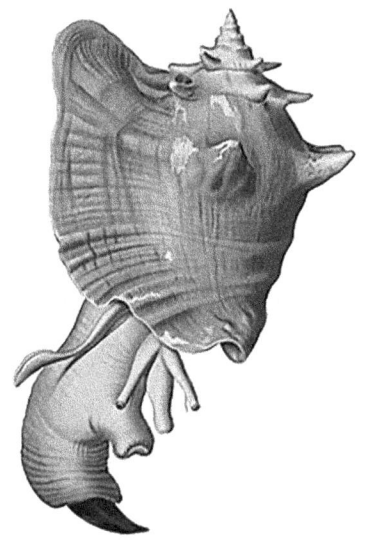

Dorsal view of an adult conch by Chenu, 1844

"**U**nderstanding and anticipation of fisherman's response to changes in biological, economic and regulatory conditions in thus critical to activities" states Bene & Tewfik (2001). Marine Resource management is multifaceted and may require various strategies to pressure conch stocks. Naturally there are some inherent issues with sampling method, however, there are some benefits such as having a selection that is representative of that an actual fishermen/ stakeholder. The mean of the sample was 15.5mm LT and the median was 15.2 mm LT. This estimate indicates that fishermen typically gather immature and mature conch as without uniformity indicated that at most stages of growth conch was extracted. With a maximum and minimum extending from 2.5mm to 33 mm. The Mean LT of 15.5mm can potentially be a regulatory size for the Bahamas which can allow juvenile conch to become mature. With 61% of the sample being determined as flared this would indicate that fishermen selection is convenience based. Stoner et. al. (2012) indicated "minimum LT for reproductive maturity was 12 mm for females and 9 mm for males, and 50%maturity for the population was achieved at 26 mm LT for females and 24 mm LT for males, higher than previous estimates. A review of fishing regulations indicates that immature queen conch are being harvested illegally in most Caribbean nations". Stoner et. al. (2012) study suggested a minimum harvest no less than of 15mm. The present research pins down on the conservative conclusion by Stoner et. al.(2012).

The results indicate both recruitment overfishing and growth overfishing. Lower Samphire was -3.1mm below the mean and when compared to Memory Rock on the t test treatment with significantly different results. Additionally, lack of uniformity in catch leads to stock depletion. With baseline evidence of recruitment overfishing. The results heavily support the idea that sexually mature conch are at greater depths both Bene and Tewfik (2001) and Stoner et. al.(2012) alluded to this proposition. Moreover, interviewed fishermen drew a similar conclusion as that seen in the study. However it would be bias to externalize both the environmental and socioeconomic factors. The Whole weight (g) also played an important role and indicates a relationship with lip thickness. Additionally, Figure 4. Indicates this relationship whereas larger weight, lip thickness at greater depths. Memory Rock (18-30ft, 16.5mm LT and 103391g) and Man-O-War Channel (33+ ft, 19.8 mm LT, and 107076g) location retained the highest depth whole weight and lip thickness. Whilst, South Long Island (6-16ft, 14.23 mm LT and 92702g) and East Booby Rocks (18-20ft, 15.15mm LT and 93469g) retained the lowest of the sample. Environmental variability, sediment organics and fishing pressure are potentially a reason for the weight of Lower Samphire. Selective fishing and the removal of adults from location these location may produce direct and indirect ecological effects on the species. Lower Samphire and Memory Rock value of the t was 3.776009. The value of p is 0.000424. The results were significant at $p ≤ 0.05$. Lower samphire lip thickness especially when compared to depth range can be indicative of fishing pressure and considering the lip thickness. Upper Samphire produced no significant difference in the t test treatment with Lower Samphire which can indicated similar environment depth range (6-18ft).

When Man-O-War Channel and East Booby Rocks lip thickness was compared in the t test the value of the t was 4.406840 and the value of p was 5.4E-05 which was significantly different when measured in $p ≤ 0.05$. Moreover when Man-O-War Channel was compared to South Long Island; the value of the t was -4.853632. The value of p was 1.2E-05. The result also significant at $p ≤ 0.05$. Man-O-War Channel compared to South Long Island; the value of the t was -4.853632. The value of p was 1.2E-05. The result is significant at $p ≤ 0.05$. Man-O-War Channel compared to Upper Samphire scores slightly lower with the value of t is -4.626149. The differentials when compared to depth may aid understanding optimal foraging techniques of the fishermen.

Titley-O' Neil et. al.(2011) suggested that once undisrupted conch mate continuously at a 1: 1 sex ratio especially during the rainy season.

Therefore if Memory Rock and Man-O-War Channel retain the greatest depth and most sexually mature species then these loactions can potential restock depleted locations (Lower Samphire, Upper Samphire and South Long Island). Understanding that Lower Samphire and Upper Samphire and South Long Island are shallow banks which require to least effort to dive, visualize, capture and transport, whilst Memory Rock & Man-O-War Channel are placed closely on shelf zone. These locations require more finances, skills and effort. This result was indicative higher productivity at these depths. the locations different mean lip thickness average may allude ton speciation or sub-species within the species of queen conch. Pressure on an isolated population may also be a factor suppressing size. Information of Catch Per Unit Effort fishermen effort may be needed to support the study.

The Environment of Upper Samphire and Lower Samphire were described as exactly the same and their lip thickness in the t test illustrates no significant difference. Considering, the depth and habit description are identical, the evidence can entail that the environments in the study are heavily encroached which indicates that lip thickness standardization is even more important (Figure 6.). Moreover, the ease of access to the environment may play a role in the level of invasion. When comparing the whole weight Man-O-War Channel compared to Memory Rock value of the t was -1.118427 and value of p was 0.2625. The result was not significant ($p ≤ 0.05$.). Figure 4 illustrates this relationship and lip thickness between the two locations. In both lip thickness and whole weight t test results were not significant. Figure 2 illustrate the limited difference between the sites with Memory Rock only at -3.29 mm less than Man-O-War Channel. The relation coincide with depth range of Memory Rock (18-30 ft) and Man-O-War Channel (33+ft). Only a 3 feet difference exist between the locations which reflects accessibility and optimal foraging especially when comparing Bene and Tewfik's(2001) socioeconomic discovery of harvest deterrents at depths conch harvest at 30ft.

Lower Samphire (1900g) weight is larger than Upper Samphire (1782 g) and East Booby Rocks (1832g) in Figure 4. Despite its smaller lip thickness. East Booby Rocks lip thickness compared to Upper Samphire as suspected value of t is -0.348037; the value of p is 0.729245. The result is not significant at $p \leq 0.05$. This may explain the differential in whole weight. Moreover, sediment organics and foraging techniques may be reason for the slightly larger weight. This concept is potentially congruent with Glazer and Kidney (2004) study in the Florida Keys. Figure 5 illustrates the lip thickness comparison over the years. Figure 5 depict a decline from 2009 to 2010 from 16.59 to 12.58 which was a – 4.01mm decline. The mean lip thickness for 2014 depicts an increase from 2010 at + 2.92 mm. Unfortunately, this might be a result of different data acquisition method. The information for 2005 to 2010 were collected from retail vendors, whilst the 2014 sample was collected directly via free diving from the ocean; 2005-2010 regression line of $R^2=0.9514$ regression line indicate a steady annual decline.

The regression line on Figure 5. Depicts a startling decrease with the result significant at (p= 0.05) (Referring to Appendix for T test Treatment values, Table1.). Therefore, if conch is continually harvested at the same rate mature stocks will continue to decline. Figure 6. Which illustrate the overspread indicate the lack of uniformity in species collection with a minimum of 2.5 mm and a maximum of 33 in 2014. The minimum of 2.5mm solidifies the concept of indiscriminate catch and the concept of optimal foraging harvest technique fishers. This indicate that fishermen a conch selection is currently on a convenience basis and therefore both mature and immature conch are amongst the catch. Implementation of a regulatory lip thickness naturally will present some issues, however, can potentially prevent encroach at all stages of conch development.

Naturally there are some inherent issues with sampling method, however, there are some benefits such as having a selection that is representative of that an actual fishermen/ stakeholder's choice. This approach allows representation day-to-day selection as catch as opposed to a scientific approach. Stoner, Davis and Booker (2012) suggested that distance to localized population may affect stock: stating that the closer the stock the greater the impacts. This research indicates distance, environmental and socio-economic factors cumulatively affect the ability of queen conch to reach sexual maturity. Additionally, challenging location to access as indicated by local fishermen were Memory Rock and Man-O-War Channel which had a greater depth requiring compressors; therefore, gas consumption, food and water and physical exertion inhibits disruption of stocks. Local fishermen (ob. 2015) described the area of Great Bahama Bank as once flourishing with a productive queen conch community and state that as time progress stocks decrease giving rise to pressure at greater distances and further locations such as the Northern Bahamas. Waves, weathering and geographical factors hinder encroachment of these stocks and allow for viable populations. However increased pressure technology usage and pressure may affect this stock replenishing promise. De Jesús-Navarrete & Valencia-Hernández (2013) analyzed the socio-economic conditions which results in encroachment. Maintaining that it is more worthwhile capturing spiny lobster (*Panilirius argus*) at such risky depth 30ft + Bene & Tewfik (2001); the annual landings value of 72 Million (Bahamian dollars) spiny lobster when compared the queen conchs 5 million (Bahamian dollars) solidify this concept (Department of Marine Resources Landing and Value Sheet, 2012).

Stoner, Davis and Booker (June, 2014) asserted these findings claiming that in the last six years the Bahamas' widely disperse fishing grounds has a trend of overfishing by locals to unsustainable reproductive levels and the density increases with distance from human communities. That would aid in explaining Man-O-War Channels and Memory Rock larger lip growth. Sample size is a typical issue in "resource selection studies (Glazer & Kidney, 2014). Queen conch has been observed at depth of 25 ft (Glazer& Kidney, 2014; Ratheir, 1993, Stoner & Schwarte, 1994, Mates et. al 1998). Gittens (ob. 2015) insist that Queen conch can be found within undisturbed pockets within the archipelago; unpressured within great abundance along the Southern Tongue of the Ocean called Sand Boors. This location is geographical difficult to navigate and dive because of rough weather and depth.

Geographic variation affects lip thickness. The depth of Man-O-War Channel is 33ft + which explains why access to the resource is more problematic. Fishing grounds with the least depth Lower Samphire (6-18ft), Upper Samphire (6-18ft) and South Long Island (6-16ft) are predominantly sandy bank community and has the least sexually mature conch sample. The depth range is less and the species are more visible. Although seasoned fishermen insist that a combination of sand shoals, coral reef and grass community. Conch aren't sessile (Bene & Tewfik, 2003); Hesse, 1979; Stoner & Sandt (1992) utilizing a "hopping" movement entitled the "strombid leap" (Parker,1922; Randall, 1964) However, daily coverable distances is limited especially due to physical barriers.

Stock decline is continuous within the Caribbean despite the use of convention the use of classical fisheries management tools; minimum size, temporal and spatial closure and total allowable catch, etc. (Bene & Tewfik, 2003). In Turks and Caicos catch per unit effort has faced a steady decline since 1991 and local fisherman are focused on remote locations within the bank (Bene & Tewfik, 2003; C. Hall ob. The Director of Environmental and Coastal Resources (DECR, 1988). Protected areas have a greater overall density; intraspecific food competition affect their growth rate is density dependent (Bene & Tewfik, 2003; Siddall, 1984). Ray and Stoner (1995) observed that daily growth rate was higher in sea grass than sand community of juveniles (2 to 5 months) therefore habitat type affect conch size and maturity (Bene & Tewfik, 2003). Natural Sand bars, land mass observed in Turks and Caicos (South East long Island side and North East Long Cay) which hindered a spillover effect and hereby inhibited by this natural enclosure (Bene & Tewfik, 2003). Sand Bar were a typical feature of the fishing ground and limit species movement from one location to the other. Therefore physical characteristic play a crucial role in size and maturity of queen conch.

Protection of spawning stocks is important to improve and maintain fishing yield (Bene & Tewfik, 2003). Spawning population can be found in deep water basin (Stoner, Davis & Booker, 2012). Therefore, extraction without control limits the capacity of reproduction; the reduction of population size and potentially influence adult reproductive activity, a relation described as the "Allee Effect". De Jesus-Navarrete & Valencia-Hernandez, 2013). Stoner, Davis & Booker (2012) studied the Allee effect recently within the Bahamas (Andros Island & Berry Islands) depicting density dependence in mating; describing habitat features, phenotypes, age, and maturity structures of queen conch population as factors affecting mating frequency. Determining factors are phenotype of adult conch, age, size. Stoner, Davis & Booker (2012) discovered the contrast within the marine protected area and fishing grounds. Conch in Exuma (Reserve) were 32%-40% larger in shell length oppose to the Berry

Islands (Fishing Ground) which where the smallest known adult species for its geographic range. Species with internal fertilization of eggs are typically density dependent to mating frequency; the location observed the minima of reproductively. Andros Island was 6.3% and Berry Island was 2.3% of mature conch when compared to Exuma Cays 12%-14% which is unfished reserved site. With density increased in Exuma Cay rating drastically increased (Stoner, Davis & Booker, 2012).

Natural size and age structure within the spawning grounds and adult density is crucial for maintaining sustainable fishing (Stoner, Davis & Booker, 2012). Man-O-War Channel and Memory Rock had older conch more sexually mature stocks. Stoner, Davis and Booker (2012) indicated that older stock tend to accumulate in deepwater which are potentially undisturbed by fishermen however, deep diving gear (SCUBA and hookah) make these remote areas accessible. The author recommended that gear be restricted. Unfortunately tis recommendation present major issues for the stakeholders. Bene and Tewfik (2001) examined artisanal fisheries and allocation of fishing effort by Fishermen in the Turks and Caicos. The authors examined some issues related to queen conch fisheries and explained that the locals prefer spiny lobster (*Panilirius argus*) and the two species are the two most exploited species. Spiny lobster hunting season in the Bahamas is closed during the reductive period of 1st April and July 31st whilst stone crab (*Menippe mercenaria*) season is closed from June 15th to October 15th. Essentially, fishermen harvest queen conch and other marine species as a substitute to financially sustain themselves during this closed period.

Spade et. al.(2010) study suggested that nearshore Queen conch might naturally have slower growth rates in nearshore habitats which can assist in describing the lip thickness of South Long Island, Upper

Samphire and Lower Samphire. Moreover, Peel and Aranda (2011) research illustrate disparate variances between countries. The present study analyze such drastic differences and recruitment overfishing may be a reason which can affect the ability of *S. gigas* to maintain a stable fishery (Stoner, Davis and Booker, 2012). Continual encroach without uniformity may further affect these locations in the future. Glazer and Kidney (2004) insist that within the Florida Keys stocks may be vulnerable to poaching because shallow water makes fishing more easier than deep sea seagrass or deep water sand plains; these deep communities can effective colonize the pressured shallow varies. In relation to the present study locations such as Man-O-War Channel and Memory Rock may be capable of colonizing more encroach shallow locations. Glazer and Kidney (2004) refer to Stoner and Ray (1996) asserting that they found many adult conch within the Bahamas in deep sand plains which predicted to evidence within this present study. The author insist a similar relationship in the U.S. Virgin Islands indicating a migratory pattern from deep waters during the year within from shallow water to deep water when the fisheries was opened and the opposite when conch fisheries was closed (Glazer & Kidney, 2004). The one common factor from this gesture is that pattern may be fishing pressure induced. Furthermore, both Venezuela population (Weil & Laughin, 1984) and Martinique (Ratheir, 1993) expressed the same shallow water to deep water patterns (Glazer and Kidney, 2004). Fishing pressure may account heavily for this discrepancy.

Glazer and Kidney (2004) observed that queen conch within the Florida Keys preferred rubble-coarse sand habitat both in reproductive and non-reproductive season; which and expected tendency since sand was the preferred reproductive ground (Glazer & Kidney, 2004; Randall, 1964; Weil & Laughin 1984; Stoner and

Sandt, 1992). Their study suggested that conch avoided these areas based on abundance and habitat proportion to its availability even in CL a site where 84% of the sample occurred in rubble. In the Caribbean and the Bahamas, however, conch reside in predominantly sea grass habitat (Randall, 1964; Weil and Laughin, 1984; De Jesus et. al., 1999; Delgado, 1999) and fishing pressure is a suggestive reason for the inconsistency (Glazer and Kidney, 2004). The sea grass within the Florida Keys is on a very "tine" substrate which is a habitat type for conch (Glazer ob., Glazer and Kidney, 2004); therefore substrate variance within the environment may also be a distribution determining factor for conch. Therefore fishing pressure and attributing factors may affect migratory pattern of *S. gigas*; with this assumption it's important to note that the substrata underlying these communities or habitats may vary between countries (Glazer & Kidney, 2004).

Bene and Twefik (2001) research on effect allocation of queen conch and spiny lobster within the Turks and Caicos indicated that within the lobster season in March cause effort to be redirected onto queen conch stocks which is evidence during the following months. Lobster which is a more lucrative target, can be found in depths of 30 ft to 50 ft with an average of 43 ft and conch ranges from 20 ft to 30 ft (Bene & Tewfik, 2001). This explains why Man-O-War Channel was less encroached. Their survey revealed incentives to preferential fishing which is related to "optimal foraging strategy" theory (Smith,1983). The optimal foraging theory in human ecology which is useful for research of hunting strategies (Bene & Tewfik, 2001) and few applied these studies to fisheries (McCay,1981 ; Beckerman, 1983; Bergossi, 1992). Different models of diet-breath, patch choice, foraging group size and time allocation etc. are all regrouped in the optimal foraging theory that are utilized in varying situations and hunting strategy question. The concept is that fishermen (predators) in a guest to maximizing landings (returns) whilst simultaneously minimizing effort (cost) (Bene & Tewfik, 2001). In the case of this research paper. The fishermen will allocate pressure to locations which the lowest cost and fishing effort (depth). Therefore extensive selection at locations such as Lower Samphire and Upper Samphire may be direct result of this choice. Conch are often have heavy shells and may be knocked out of their shells at sea, the weight of the shell require more effort and gas to arrive to and from the location.

Mariculture Potential

Conch research and mariculture was spearheaded in the Bahamas due to general consensus that stocks where declining. It was first suggested by Brownell (1977) approximately 40 years ago that hatcheries would 'augment' and replenish dwindling conch population within the Western Atlantic. Limited migration, habitats, high fecundity and market demand all lead lead to the concept of conch mariculture. Randall, 1964; Alcodocko, 1976 and Bery, 1976; Brownell, et. al, 1977 all meeting for stimulus and increased reserved it's potential with relatively small amounts of expectation Wallace Groves Aquaculture Foundation in Freeport (Bahamas) was the first to increase it's study in 1980 throughout the Western Atlantic area. This resulted in investment by the University of Miami (Miami Florida, U. S.) which was lead by Iverson and his co-workers in the Berry Island Bahamas whilst in Venezuela, Los Roques Archipelago Laughinconducted studies with his peers, in the University of Puerto Rico, Appledorn and his co-worker conducted studies; in the Turks and Caicos, Hesse and Davis and peers conducted studies inPuerto Morelos (QuintanaRoo, Mexico) conch project and finally in the U.S. Virgin Islands Coulston et. al 1987 conducted research. Lack of finances was the major reason for the lack of investment in research of conch mariculture. Other places such as MercidaYacatan Mexico, Lee Stocking Island by the Caribbean Marine Research Center (Veno Beach, Florida, U. S. A.) by Stoner and co-worker the Florida Keys, by the Florida Institute of Marine Research (Glazer and Berg, 1994). The first main issue with mariculture is the inability to produce consistent high membrane of juvenile for restocking which was discovered at the University of Miami and the Berry Island (Bahamas) (Sidall, 1983). High mortality is another because when released into the wild there is high predation. Predation is the highest cause of natural mortality mainly in organism under 1 year of age (Iverson et. al, 1986) which is a determinate of stock restocking success or failure. Availability to efficient date of catch per unit effort which may go hand in hand with information of the biology of the species (Iverson and Jory,1997). Iverson and Jory, 1997 states " restocking suitable environments with hatchery- reserved juveniles to re-established or augment a stock or population is a technique that has been attempted with many species including numerous mollusk; mussels, abalone, cockles, quahogs, bay scallops, tridacnid clams, oysters and queen conch (Jory et. al, 1984; Karney, 1994). Extensive research has been done on the abalone and released from hatcheries all around the world such as California and British Columbia have shown the rare results as issue as conch. Survival on conch in hatcheries within the Caribbean is extremely low the information collected in the Bahamas indicate a relationship between size and survivorability. In Venezuela, Los Roques after rearing 10 conch cultures through metamorphisis during 1981; however in 1982 attempts to rear 60 culture resulted in fails and the cultures resulted in fails and the cultures, Miami and Bonaire have resulted in failures. The only consistently successful conch hatchery since the 1980's is the Turkand Caicos but their commercial grow out are still not successful (Iverson and Jory, 1997). Furthermore, it was discovered in the Berry Island that penned conch grow much slower than wild species (Iverson et. Al, 1987) because of less physical activity and less conch density; furthermore conch shell formation was discovered to have a relationship with physical activity and hence capture conch shell would grow much slower (Iverson and Jory 1987). Mariculture has potential and with adequate research and financial resources it may be able to augment stock decline.

Replenishing the population

Populations of queen conch is below the critical threshold for reproduction and is rapidly declining within the Caribbean nations and Florida. Attempts to utilize hatcheries have also been unsuccessful in Florida, Mexico, Puerto Rico and the Bahamas in an attempt to augment stock decline and rebuild stocks (Stoner, Davis & Booker, 2011). Conch mariculture in the Bahamas has potential it there would have to offshore penned sites all well as near shore hatcheries in order for this concept to work. Therefore there must be transplantations of stocks which would allow the thin shell slow growing conch in the near shore environment to be moved to offshore environment where it can grow much faster. The first initial strategy may be to form a season for conch: this leads to a variety of issue since stone crab (Menippemercenaria) closed season is from June 15th to October 15th and spiny lobster during (Panulirusargus)April 1 to July 31, whilst Nassau grouper (Epinephelusstriatus) December 1st - February 28th . Therefore it would be difficult implementing a season without stakeholder approval and prior to that the time frames may clash which negatively affects those fisherman who hunt for conch when crawfish or grouper season is closed. Research in both Northern and Southern Bahamas conch flip size would aid in a settlement on conch lip size. The operculum can also be studied and utilized for the vessel that don't return with the conch's shell, however, sufficient studies must be carried out first. Admittedly, there is a vast variety of inefficacies in strategies presented. Therefore a thorough revaluation of these strategies must take place. Therefore the entire countries lip size need to be measured in outer to find the common size of each location. Moreover the gonado-stomatic indices also should be a priority. Outer issue also persist and that is seen within the marine reserve and this indicates that sufficient funding should be placed on research and conservation of several marine reserves as oppose to creating new reserves and stretching the resources thin. Creating resources based on ecological significance may also be an important criteria which is seen in the area of Middle Bight, North Bite and Grassy Cay. Stoner et al (2012) concluded that the Exuma Land and Sea Park has reach reproductive inefficacy which is why stronger management ad greater resources must be placed on their significant location. The Department of Marine Resources faces various limitation that result in a variety of inefficacies; Stoner, Davis and Booker (2009) stated,"Unfortunately, finding for stock density in the Bahamas has not been available and DOMR is without data to make informed decisions." This means that they are hindered by limited resource and hence they are unable tomake decisions based on statistical data. In the final analysis it would take a mosaic of funding and strategies to allow for proper management of the large marine gastropod.

Shells at Montagu

Areil View of conch shell middens (Monique Willaims)

CONCLUSION

In the Bahamas fisheries management is mono-fishery based approach. Unfortunately, this form of management focuses on stock and not the interaction between exploited stocks and human activities; therefore, fishermen behavioral patterns should be given the same degree of attention as stock assessment or population dynamics and marine ecology. Bene and Tewfik (2001) quotes Hilborn assertions (1985 p. 3) "a major element of fisheries science should be the study of fishermen and fleet dynamics". The present research discovered this factor was a predominant issue and Bene and Tewfik (2001) 15 years after Hilborn (1985 p. 3) assert their traces of the information however, the majority was excluded and "desperately low". Additionally, Iverson & Jory (1997) states that data collection isn't unique to Small Island Developing States it is more prevalent in those countries. Moreover mono-fishery approach cannot control or describe fishery effort and logistics. A standardize lip thickness would aid in the development of uniformity and may limit stock depletion. The pressure on the Bahamian market increase due to closure in other Caribbean islands. Fishing quota on high spawning area and a standardize lip thickness of 15mm are all potential option to control fishing effort. However, in debt research should be done involving stalking holder input, simulation models are all necessary before these steps. Stock assessment should also be addressed as well. Therefore, the future of conch fisheries may be dependent on uniform management.

The Department of Marine Resources is a government agency that of which is responsible for a variety of surrounding fisheries and ecosystems management, task of which may involve the protect and regulation of marine resources, data collection, policy creation and legislation, education and awareness etc. Species specific management plan is nothing new to Small Island Developing States and is certainly nothing new to the Bahamas sense every niche area within fisheries has a regulatory management plan. The generation of such a plan that would lead the Bahamas Marine Resources Potentially for the next five to 10 years and obtaining the financial resources to assist such a duress endeavor is only half the skirmish. One criteria for a fisheries management plan is that it is 3D, defendable, divestible, definable, and requires equal division of natural rights. Venezuela closed its queen conch fisheries in 1991 which allowed the stocks to be replenished. One potential is to end all exports of the valuable fisheries product. This concept was recommended by the Bahamas Department of Marine Resources (DMR) to end the external distribution of the resource, however the bill has yet to be politically enacted despite the fact that the large gastropod is a part of the CITES appendix (ii). Marine reserves, quotas and other management strategies are important are significant however it is even more crucial to determine the genetic connectivity amongst conch stocks which assist with determination of appropriate recruitment stock in the complex marine environment. Moreover in 2009 conch exceeded its export quota in 2009. The information regarding the relationship between total stocks and exports have yet to be calibrated and hence a figurative result hasn't officially been established and hence ending its international transport is inhibited. Stoner et al 2012 states that " given the limitations that all the management tools discussed above, it seems likely that specific controls on total fishing mortality will be required for sustainable fishery. Currently, an export quota for queen conch exist in the Bahamas, and while accurate records for total catch are not available because of the dispersed nature of the conch fisheries, conch intended for export are estimated to make up one half of the total catch. For long term sustainability ending the export market might be wise, leaving the product for domestic consumption only". Another option would be to add taxes to the export of the species which has been implemented in Jamaica at 1$ per pound. Moreover the finances gained can be utilized at the Department of Marine Resources to increase management capacity (Stoner, Davis and Booker, 2011). Furthermore, implementations such as a Maximum Sustainable Catch (MSC) for all queen conch may be easily accepted but it may require other management strategies to maintain the framework for its implementation. Furthermore a sustainable conch lip size could be initiated for restaurants and fish houses which is where most fisherman sell their products. This strategy may induce the implementation of new markets however it be more effective than a MSC certification. The integration of both stakeholder groups, exporter and local communities may also be an effective strategy to sustain the fisheries; lobbies are proven to be very successful in determining the political agendas and hence these individual can be a catalyst for preserving the fishery. Education and awareness campaigns have also been proficient in safeguarding the fishery. Long-term growth of the mariculture industry in the Bahamas depends on both ecologically sound practices and sustainable resource management. Governments can encourage such practices by stringently regulating the creation of new farming facilities in mangroves and other coastal wetlands, establishing fines to minimize escapes of fish from aquaculture pens, enforcing strict disease control measures for the movement of stock, and mandating effluent treatment and in pond recirculation of wastewater. Many aquaculture operations have adopted such practices even in the absence of strict government policies, especially with the heightening of environmental concerns in recent years. In our countries, however, such policies are often neither politically enforceable nor economically and socially feasible. On the public side, governments can support research and development on environmentally benign aquaculture systems, eliminate implicit subsidies for ecologically unsound practices, and establish and enforce regulations to protect coastal ecosystems. At the same time, the private sector must alter its course and recognize that current practices that lead to further pressures on ocean fish stocks, destruction of coastal habitats, water pollution, and introductions of pathogens and non-native fish run counter to the industry's long-term health. If public and private interests act jointly to reduce the environmental costs generated by conch farming, present unsustainable trends can be reversed and aquaculture can make an increasingly positive contribution to global fish supplies. Without this shared vision, however, an expanded aquaculture industry poses a threat, not only to ocean fisheries, but also to itself. Although world fish production from capture fisheries leveled off during the 1990s, demand for seafood continues to increase. This is because of the growth of the human population and also the view that seafood is healthy food. Scientists believe that natural production from the ocean will not increase; consequently, if the demand for seafood by humans is to be met in the future, both mariculture and fresh-water aquaculture production will have to increase significant. Evidently there is no clear solution to the management of conch which why holistic management strategies must be implemented.

ACKNOWLEDGEMENT

A special thanks is extended to Lester Gittens and the Department of Marine Resources for the data to be analyzed for the study. Mr. Lionel Johnson, Lester Flowers and William Fielding advisors (College of the Bahamas) assistance was also gracefully accepted. Local Fishermen such as Jeff Jolly inputs to data are also gracefully accepted and future and the plan is to build relationships for future research in the marine resources area.

(Note that although the conch on the left is smaller it is mature as opposed to the larger of whom lip isn't flared)

Photo by Schlochtern,M M(2014)

REFERENCES

Avila-Poveda, H. O., Baquero-Cardenas, E. R. (2006) Size and Maturity in the Queen Conch *Strombus gigas* from Columbia. *Bol. Invert. Mari. Cost.* ISSN 0122-9761.

Teiley-Oneal, C. P., Macdonald, B. A., Pelleter, E., Saint-Loius, R. & Phillip, O. S. (2011) The Relationship Between Imposex and Tributyltin (TBT) Concentration in *Strombus gigas* from the British Virgin Islands. *Bulletin of Marine Science.* D.O.I. 10.5343

Glazer, R.A. & Kidney, J.A. (2004) Habitat Association of Adult Queen Conch (*Strombus gigas L.*) in an Unfish Florida Keys Back Reef: Application of Essentail Fish Habitat. Bulletin of Marine Science, 75(2): 205-224

Jesus-Navarette, A.D. & Valencia-Henendez, A. (2013) Declining densisties and reproductive activities of the Queen Conch *Strombus gigas* (Mesogastropoda: Strombidae) in Banco Chinchoro, Eastern Caribbean, Mexico. Rev. Biol. Trop. Vol. 61 (4): 1671-1679

Bene, C. & Tewfik, A. (2001) Fishing Effort Allocation and Fishermen's Decision Making Processs in a Multi-Species Small-Scale Fishery Analalysis of Conch and Lobster Fishery in Turks and Caicos Islands. *Human Ecology.* Vol. 29, No. 2 pg 157-186.

Peel, J.R. and Arnada, D.A. (2011) Growth and Population Assessment of the Queen Conch *Strombus gigas* (Mesogastropoda: Strombidae) by capture mark-recapture sampling in natural protected area of the Mexican Caribbean. REl. Biol. Trop. ISSN-0034-7744.

Christope, B., Tewif, A. (2003). Biological Evaluation of Marine Protected Area: Evidence of Crowding Effect on a Population pf Queen Conch in the Caribbean. *Marine Ecology.* 24. 1: 45-58, 14p. DOI: 10.1046/ 1. 1439-0485. 2003.03782.x

Danylchuk, A. J. (2005). Fisheries Management in South Eleuthera Bahamas: Can a Marine Reserve Help Save the 'Holy Trinity'. *Gulf and Caribbean Fisheries Institute.* 56

Iverson, E. S. & Jory, D. E. (1997). Mariculture and Enhancement of Wild Populations of Queen Conch *Strombus Gigas. Bulletin of Marine Science.* 60(3): 929- 941.

Muller, K. W. & Stoner, A.W.,(2013) Proxy measures for Queen Conch (*Strombus gigas*, Linne, 1758) Age of Maturity: Relationships between shell Lip thickness and Operculum Dimensions. *Journal of Shellfish.* 32, 789-744

Schapira, D., Montano, A. I., Antezak, A.& Posada, M. J. (2009). Using shell middens to asses effects of fishing on queen conch (*Strombus gigas*) populations in Los Roques Archipelago National Park, Venezuela. *Marine Biology.* 156, 787-795. DOI: 10.10071s00227-009-1133-1

Schweizer, D., Posada, J. M.,(2002). Distribution, Density and Abundance of the Queen Conch, *Strombus gigas*, in the Los Roques Archipelago National Park Venezuela. *Gulf and Caribbean Fisheries Institute.* 53

Spade, J. D., Griffith, R. J., Lui, L., Brown-Peterson, N.J., Kroll, K. J., Feswick, A., Glazer, R. A., Barber, D.S., Denslow, N. D. (2010). Queen Conch (*Strombus gigas*) Testis Regresses during the Reproductive Season at Near shore Sites in the Florida Keys. *Plos one* 5, 9, e12737

Stoner, A.W., Mueller, K.W., Brown-Peterson, N. J., Davis, M. H., Booker, C. J. (2012). Maturation and age in queen conch (*Strombus gigas*): Urgent needs for changes in harvest criteria. *Fisheries Research.* 131-133: 76-84.

Stoner, A. W., Davis, M. H., Booker, C. J. (2012). Abundance and population structure of queen conch inside and outside a marine protected area: repeat surveys how significant declines. *Marine Ecology Progress Series.* 460: 101-114.

Stoner, A. W., Davis, M. H., Booker, C. J. (2012). Negative consequences of Allee Effects are Compounded by Fishing pressure: Comparison of Queen conch reproduction in Fishing grounds and a Marine Protected Area. *Bulletin of Marine Science.* 88: 1 : 89-104.

Stoner, A., Davis M. & Booker C.(2009) Queen Conch Stock Assessment: Proposed MPA and Fishing Grounds Berry Island, Bahamas. *Community Conch*

Stoner, A., Davis M. & Booker C. States of Knowledge of Conch Resources in the Bahamas and Management Considerations (2011). *Community Conch*

Wilson, S. K., Street, S. and Sato, T. (2005). Discarded queen conch (*Strombus gigas*) shell as shelter sites for fish. *Marine Biology* (2005) 147, 179-188. DOI: 10.10071s00227-005-1556-2

Brumbaugh, Daniel R (ed.) 2014. Guide to the Science of Marine Protect Areas in the Bahamas. American Museum of Natural History, New York, NY 16pp. retrieved http.//bbp.amnh.org

APPENDIX

Table 5 Illustrating Significance of Figure 5.

Years	T-value	P-Value	significant at p < .05
2005 & 2006	2.189265	.014431	YES
2005 & 2008	4.822632	< .00001	YES
2005 & 2009	5.953982	< .00001	YES
2005 & 2010	6.907865	< .00001	YES
2006 & 2008	2.069951	.019388	YES
2006 & 2009	2.836158	.002328	YES
2006 & 2010	4.563531	< .00001	YES
2008 & 2009	0.731563	.232291	NO
2009 & 2010	2.859516	.002169	YES

Table 6 Illustrating Sample Size of Figure 5.

Year	2005	2006	2008	2009	2010
Sample Size	487	330	481	679	239

Figure 4.

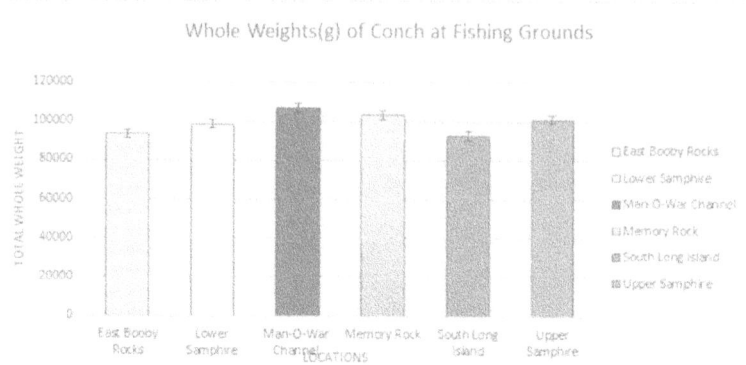

The Whole Weight of Conch was demonstrated at each Fishing Grounds

The Following Tables illustrate the Breakdown for 2005-2010

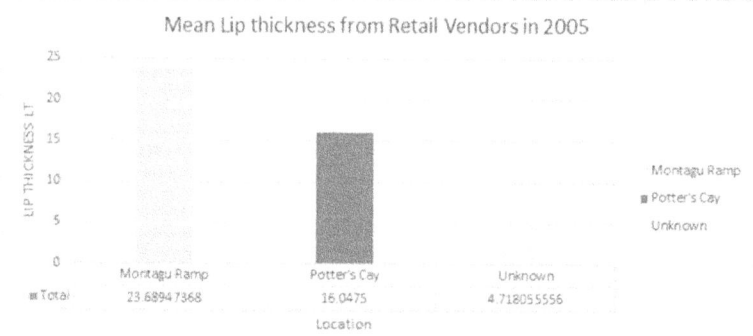

The Fall of Conch Fisheries

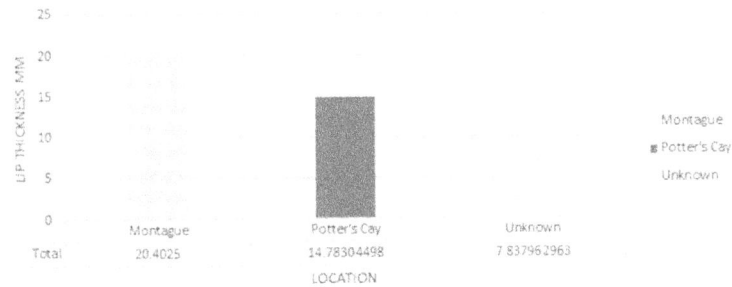

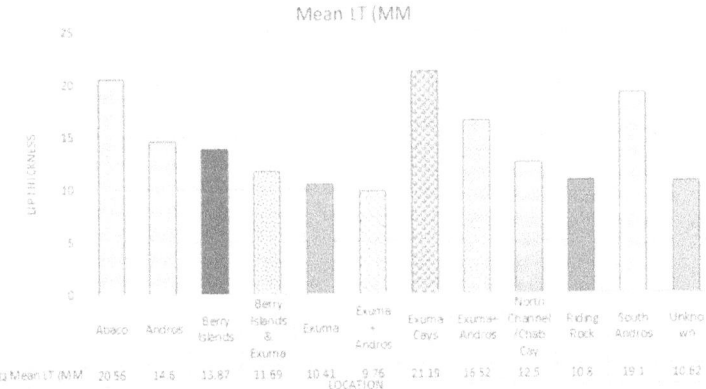

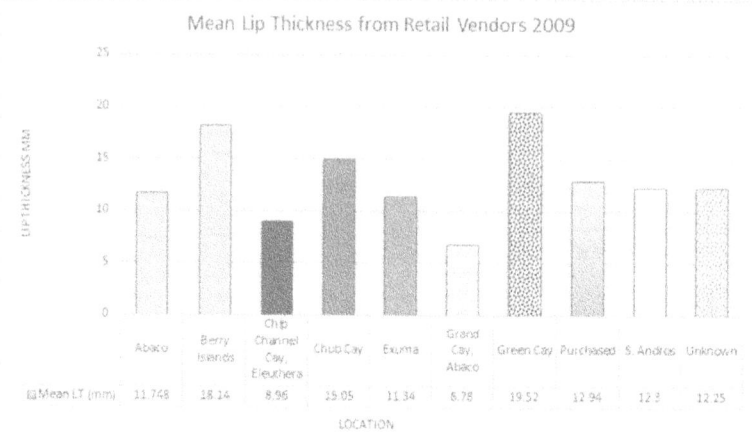

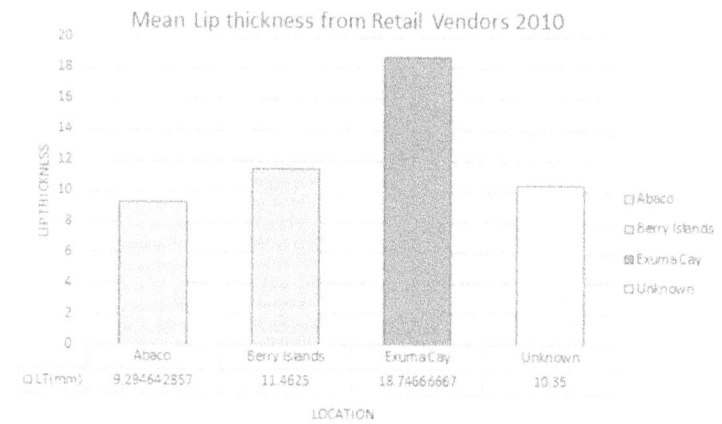

Table 3. Box plot statistics (Relates to Figure 7)

	Male	Female	Unsexed
Upper whisker	33.00	28.00	25.00
3rd quartile	21.00	18.40	20.55
Median	16.00	15.00	15.40
1st quartile	12.00	10.66	13.00
Lower whisker	3.00	2.50	6.00
Nr. of data points	120.00	178.00	15.00

Table 4. Box plot statistics (Explains Figure 8)

	Male	Female	Unsexed
Upper whisker	2608.18	2608.18	2069.53
3rd quartile	2069.52	2069.51	2041.16
Median	1927.77	1871.09	1899.44
1st quartile	1700.98	1700.98	1814.39
Lower whisker	1219.03	1247.39	1502.54
Nr. of data points	120.00	177.00	14.00

Table 5. Box plot Statistics of Lip Thickness at Fishing Grounds (relates to Fig9

	EBR	LS	MOW	MR	SLI	US
Upper whisker	23.00	27.30	28.50	26.00	23.00	28.30
3rd quartile	18.15	16.50	23.75	18.75	19.00	18.45
Median	15.20	12.10	21.00	17.00	12.50	14.70
1st quartile	11.65	8.30	17.50	13.50	10.50	10.30
Lower whisker	4.70	2.80	12.00	6.00	8.00	4.10
Nr. of data points	52.00	51.00	52.00	51.00	52.00	52.00

Figure 7.

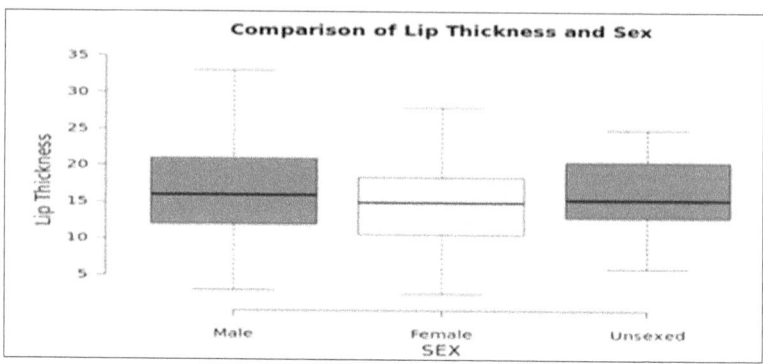

Figure 7. Indicates thickness variation between sexes.

Figure 8.

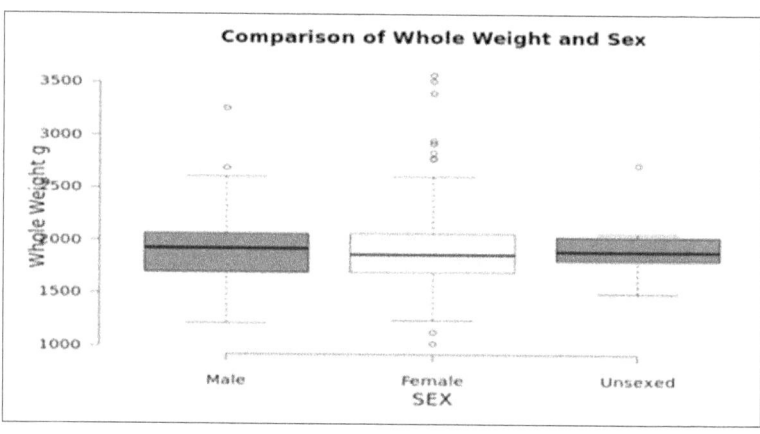

The results of weight in the box plot was insignificant.

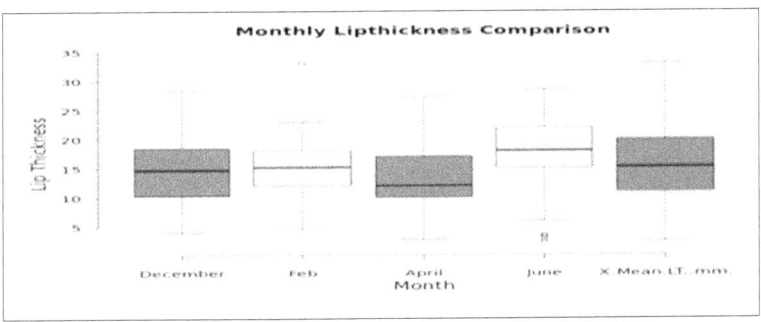

Table 5. Box Plot Statistics during Months

	December	Feb	April	June	Mean LT mm
Upper whisker	28.30	23.00	27.30	28.50	33.00
3rd quartile	18.45	18.10	17.00	22.00	20.00
Median	14.70	15.20	12.05	18.00	15.20
1st quartile	10.30	12.10	10.00	15.00	11.00
Lower whisker	4.10	4.70	2.80	6.00	2.50
Nr. of data points	52.00	53.00	102.00	106.00	313.00

Table 6. Box plot statistics (Fig 10)

	EBR	LS	MOW	MR	SLI	US
Upper whisker	2154.58	2523.13	2438.06	2579.83	2324.66	2608.18
3rd quartile	1899.44	2055.36	2154.56	2140.41	1941.94	2112.06
Median	1871.09	1842.74	2041.16	1956.14	1842.72	1941.96
1st quartile	1700.98	1587.59	1927.77	1828.56	1587.57	1700.98
Lower whisker	1417.49	1027.00	1644.27	1417.49	1219.03	1133.99
Nr. of data points	51.00	52.00	52.00	52.00	52.00	52.00

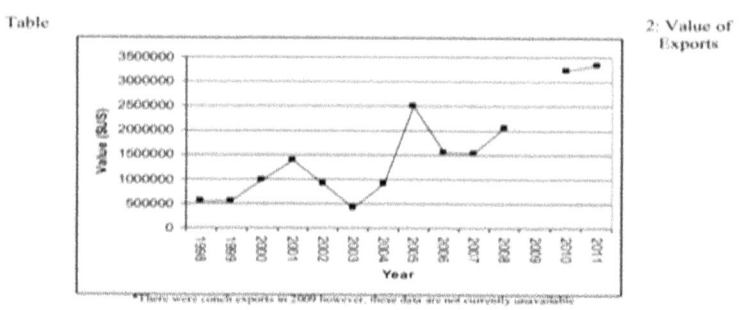

Gittens & Braynen (2012)

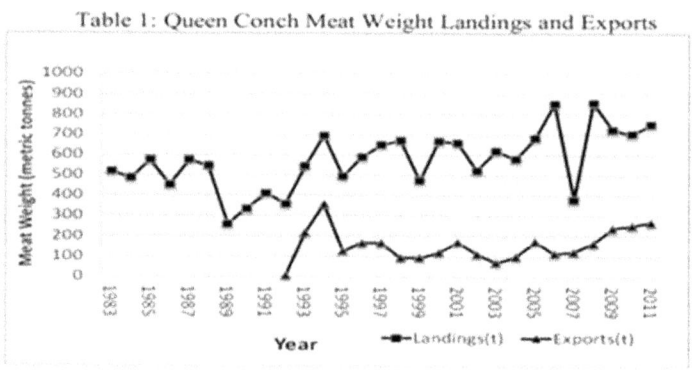

Gittens & Braynen (2012)

Table 9
Shell length (SL) and shell lip thickness (LT) parameters observed for maturity in queen conch in different parts of the greater Caribbean region. Values represent the minimum measures where maturity was observed (SL_{min}, LT_{min}) and where 50% of the population sampled was sexually mature (SL_{50}, LT_{50}) based upon histological evaluation of ovaries and testes.

Location	SL_{min} – female (mm)	SL_{min} – male (mm)	LT_{min} – female (mm)	LT_{min} – male (mm)	Reference
San Andres Archipelago, Providencia, & Santa Catalina, Colombia	205	~214	2	8	Avila-Poveda and Baquero-Cárdenas (2006)
San Andres Archipelago, Colombia	~170	~170	~5	~5	Aldana-Aranda and Frenkiel (2007)
Barbados	~260	~260	3	3	Bissada (2011)
Exuma Cays, Bahamas	176	179	12	9	This study

Location	SL_{50} – female (mm)	SL_{50} – male (mm)	LT_{50} – female (mm)	LT_{50} – male (mm)	Reference
San Andres Archipelago, Providencia, & Santa Catalina, Colombia	249	234	17.5	13.0	Avila-Poveda and Baquero-Cárdenas (2006)
Barbados	282	280	18.8	19.2	Bissada (2011)
Exuma Cays, Bahamas	206	210	26.3	24.0	This study

$LT < 10$ mm LT are reproductively active, and that individuals with $LT > 15$ mm contribute most to reproductive output.

GMI increased generally with GSI for both females and males; however, the correlations were weak and probably not meaningful.

Pearson correlation coefficients for females and males were 0.409 and 0.494, respectively.

4. Discussion

TABLE 4
Comparative Table of mean growth rates of *S. gigas*

Author, Year	Location	Method	Growth rate (mm month⁻¹)	Growth rate (mm day⁻¹)
Randall 1964	Virgin Islands, USA	Enclosure	4.16	~0.136
Alcolado 1976	Cuba	Enclosure, different environments	3.3	~0.108
Brownell 1977	Florida Keys, USA	Enclosure	4.5	~0.147
Gibson et al. 1983	Belize	Mark-Recapture	7.2	~0.236
Weil & Laughlin 1984	Venezuela	Mark-Recapture	15	~0.492
Ray & Stoner 1994	Exuma Cays, Bahamas	Enclosure	–	0.058–0.139
De Jesús-Navarrete & Oliva-Rivera 1997	Punta Gavilán, Mexico	Mark-Recapture	10	~0.327
De Jesús-Navarrete 2001	Banco Chinchorro, Mexico	Enclosure, different environments	3.21	~0.1052
De Jesús-Navarrete 2002	Punta Gavilán, Mexico	Enclosure, different environments	2.30	~0.075
Moreno de la Torre & Aldana-Aranda 2005	Mexico	Laboratory conditions, artificial diet	–	0.16–0.23

Avila- Poveda (2006) Santa Marta Columbia.

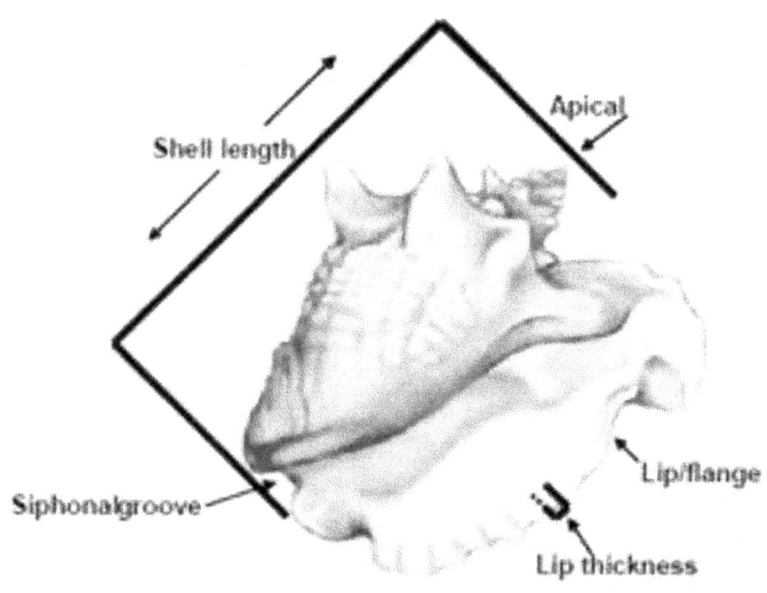

Photo by Schlochtern,M M(2014)

www.ingramcontent.com/pod-product-compliance
Ingram Content Group UK Ltd.
Pitfield, Milton Keynes, MK11 3LW, UK
UKHW022216230426
12048UKWH00016BA/881